"It is with a sense of relief that I turn from the amateurish and even wrong-headed writings of the 'openness' theologians to this work by John Frame. He is as much at home in the historical dimensions of the debate as in the theological; he is as much in command of the interpretation of the relevant biblical texts as he is of the philosophical issues. With its wholly admirable freshness and a crisp incisiveness, this book is something both to read and to give away to friends. A sad mark of the theological ignorance of our times is that Socinianism can dress itself up in new terminology and pass itself off as evangelical theology instead of a pernicious error frequently and roundly condemned. Frame's antidote is both needed and effective." —D. A. CARSON

"Open theism is bad news. The appearance of this book is good news. Precisely because God is closed and not open to the nullification of his purposes (Job 42:2), he has opened a future for believers that is utterly secure no matter what we suffer. The key that would open the defeat of God is eternally closed within the praiseworthy vault of his precious sovereignty. With the Bible as his criterion, John Frame delights to show when it is good to be closed and when it is good to be open." —JOHN PIPER

"We have known that John Frame is a superb theologian. In this book we discover that he is a superb polemicist. Here he responds to one of the most alluring trends in modern evangelicalism. He does so thoroughly, fairly, and most of all, with a convincing alternative. Frame builds the biblical case for a God whose sovereignty is something not to be avoided, but cherished." —WILLIAM EDGAR

"John Frame's *No Other God* presents the serious minded, biblically faithful, and philosophically responsible reflections of a seasoned theologian regarding the profoundly misguided open view of God. While portions of Frame's criticism could be directed more generally to classic Arminianism's commitments to libertarian freedom and the centrality of the love of God, yet much of Frame's deepest concern focuses upon a range of distinctively and deeply distressing aspects of the post-Arminian openness model. Here one will see vividly so much that is wrong with open theism while encountering afresh the beauty and glory of the true and living God of the Bible." —BRUCE A. WARE

"In my judgment 'open theism,' with its denial of God's advance knowledge of future decisions of 'free' moral agents, is a cancer on evangelicalism. Since radiation and chemotherapy have not worked so far, the time has come for surgery. Professor Frame has demonstrated excellent qualifications for this operation. His appeal to Scripture is excellent, and he has provided a devastating critique of the concept of human freedom as articulated in the 'open theistic' view." —ROGER NICOLE

"Drawing upon years of study of the doctrine of God, Frame has written a defense of the orthodox understanding of God and a response to open theism that is clear, fair, learned, and profound." —DANIEL DORIANI

"Combining exegetical good judgment, sound theology, and profound philosophical insight, Professor Frame has written exactly the book we need today to put into the hands of Christians attracted to the allegedly 'new' doctrines of so-called open theism. Open theism leaves believers with a god who is not merely 'too small' but irrelevant to our lives, our needs, our goals. And John Frame spells this out clearly in this easy-to-read but comprehensive and compelling critique. It is 'must reading' for all Christians today." —ROBERT B. STRIMPLE

No Other
God

NO OTHER GOD

A RESPONSE TO OPEN THEISM

JOHN M. FRAME

P&R

PUBLISHING

P.O. BOX 817 • PHILLIPSBURG • NEW JERSEY 08865-0817

Page design and typesetting by Lakeside Design Plus

Printed in the United States of America

Library of Congress Cataloging-in-Publication Data

Frame, John M., 1939–
    No other God : a response to open theism / John M. Frame.
        p.   cm.
    Includes bibliographical references and indexes.
    ISBN 0-87552-185-1 (pbk.)
    1. God. 2. Theology, Doctrinal. I. Title.
    BT102.F755   2001
    231—dc21

                                                            2001034021

To the board, faculty,
administration, students, and staff of
Reformed Theological Seminary

Contents

Preface 11

1. What Is Open Theism? 15

The Rhetoric and the Reality
The Openness of the Sovereign God
Sovereign Vulnerability
The Ambiguities of Open Theism
The Open-Theist View of Traditional Theism
The Main Contentions of Open Theism

2. Where Does Open Theism Come From? 25

The Antiquity of Open Theism
God and the Greeks
Socinianism: the Missing Link in Open Theism's
      Genealogy
More Recent Influences
What Is New About Open Theism?

3. How Do Open Theists Read the Bible? 41

Logic
Models
Straightforward Exegesis and Anthropomorphism

4. **Is Love God's Most Important Attribute?**   49

    Love, Sensitivity, Responsiveness, and Vulnerability

5. **Is God's Will the Ultimate Explanation
   of Everything?**   57

    The Natural World
    Human History
    Individual Human Lives
    Human Decisions
    Sins
    Faith and Salvation
    Summary Passages

6. **How Do Open Theists Reply?**   89

    Universalizing Particulars?
    Divine Foreordination Versus Human Responsibility?
    What Kind of Election?
    How Can God Act "Now" If He Acts "Always"?
    Other Open-Theist Objections

7. **Is God's Will Irresistible?**   105

    Antecedent and Consequent Wills
    Decretive and Preceptive Wills
    Sanders's Distinction
    The Efficacy of God's Will

8. **Do We Have Genuine Freedom?**   119

    A Critique of Libertarianism
    Other Kinds of Freedom
    The Problem of Evil

9. **Is God in Time?**   143

    Arguments Against Divine Atemporality

Philosophical Arguments for Divine Supratemporality
Scripture on God and Time
God's Temporal Omnipresence

10. **Does God Change?**   161

A God Who Relents
How Is God Unchanging?
Unchangeability and Temporal Omnipresence

11. **Does God Suffer?**   179

Aseity
Does God Have Feelings?
Is God Ever Weak?
Does God Suffer Death in Christ?

12. **Does God Know Everything in Advance?**   191

Divine Ignorance in Scripture?
God's Exhaustive Knowledge of the Future

13. **Is Open Theism Consistent with Other Biblical Doctrines?**   205

Biblical Inspiration
Sin
Redemption
Assurance
Heaven and Hell
Guidance

14. **Conclusion**   211

Bibliography   213

Index of Scripture   221

Index of Names and Subjects   229

Preface

The purpose of this book is to describe and evaluate biblically the theological movement known as open theism. Open theists teach that God is not above time, that he does not control all of nature and history, that he does not know the future exhaustively, that he sometimes makes mistakes and changes his plans, and therefore that he is in some ways dependent on the world. Open theists present their views winsomely and have attracted many disciples. But, in my judgment, their position is deeply unbiblical, and their movement has caused division and confusion in churches, seminaries, colleges, publishing houses, and other Christian organizations.[1]

In my much larger book, *The Doctrine of God* (forthcoming), I deal in various places with these issues and, to a lesser extent, with open theism itself. But my critique there is scattered over many chapters that also deal with other subjects, which may make it difficult for readers to gather it all together. Since the subject of open theism is so very important in our time, I have brought my thoughts together on that the-

---

1. Bruce A. Ware documents at length the controversy within the Baptist General Conference, in *God's Lesser Glory* (Wheaton, Ill.: Crossway Books, 2000), 21–27, and there cites other examples of the inroads of open theism.

ological movement in this smaller book. This book contains some material from *The Doctrine of God*, but also quite a bit of new material that responds specifically to the writings of the open theists and looks more deeply into relevant biblical texts.

Although my general evaluation of open theism is negative, I have benefited from my interaction with open theists. They have challenged me to better understand the "give-and-take" between God and the world described in the Bible. I agree with the open theists that we cannot simply write off this give-and-take as anthropomorphism. Or, if we choose to call these descriptions anthropomorphic, we need to give closer attention to the meaning of *anthropomorphic* in this connection. So I try, in this book, not only to criticize open theism, but also to formulate the relationship between God's eternal plan and the events of creation more precisely than traditional theists have sometimes done.

In this book, therefore, there is some give-and-take between the open theists and myself. I have tried to be fair in my interpretation of their writings, to avoid caricature, to give credit where credit is due, and to acknowledge weaknesses where they exist in the traditional position. I trust that my negative criticism will be all the stronger for that.

I'm thankful to all who have encouraged me in this project (and in my writing of the parent volume, *The Doctrine of God*) and who have shared their thoughts with me on these subjects. My esteemed senior colleague, Roger Nicole, has been especially helpful in sharing material both from his own writings and from those of others. I should say, too, that after I completed the first draft of this book, Bruce Ware's excellent *God's Lesser Glory: The Diminished God of Open Theism* became available.[2] After I read it, I had second thoughts about my own work: what could I add to a treatment as full, balanced, and

2. See the previous footnote.

persuasive as Ware's? But third thoughts have prevailed: I believe now that I can contribute some things, both to the foundation and to the superstructure of Ware's argument, as his enthusiastic fellow worker, without detracting from his achievement. Among other things, I give more attention than Ware does to (1) the universality of divine sovereignty, (2) the unscripturality and incoherence of the libertarian view of human freedom, (3) the metaphysical and epistemological presuppositions of open theism, and (4) the movement's historical background. As I look over my manuscript, I find that, although Ware and I share many concerns and ideas, one who reads both books will not notice much repetition. And, apart from any differences between our two treatments, Ware should have company. It is important to gather multiple witnesses in defense of what we believe to be the biblical position.

Thanks also to P&R Publishing for their quick expression of willingness to support this effort, and to my students at Westminster Theological Seminary in California and Reformed Theological Seminary in Orlando for their stimulating interaction. Especially, I am thankful to my student Justin Taylor for bibliographic suggestions and for his comments on an early draft of this volume, and to James Scott, who edited this volume on behalf of P&R. Also, thanks to Canon Press for their permission to include parts of my article, "Open Theism and Divine Foreknowledge,"[3] and generally for cheering me on.

---

3. Forthcoming in *Bound Only Once: The Openness of God as a Failure of Imagination, Nerve, and Reason,* edited by Douglas Wilson, to be published by Canon Press.

ONE

What Is Open Theism?

In this chapter, I shall try to describe the open-theist position in general terms, contrasting it with traditional theism. But first I need to clear away some barriers to mutual understanding.

The Rhetoric and the Reality

Open theists have not always been clear in describing what they believe. Many (though certainly not all) of their expositions are more like motivational talks or political speeches than philosophy or serious theology. They seem to be more interested in persuasion than clarity. They often write emotive prose, calculated to give the reader a good feeling about their position and a bad feeling about traditional views of God. I must begin by warning readers not to let themselves be carried away with this rhetoric.

For example, the open theist Clark Pinnock distinguishes "two models of God" that people "commonly carry around in their minds":

> We may think of God primarily as an aloof monarch, removed from the contingencies of the world, unchangeable

in every aspect of being, as an all-determining and irresistible power, aware of everything that will ever happen and never taking risks. Or we may understand God as a caring parent with qualities of love and responsiveness, generosity and sensitivity, openness and vulnerability, a person (rather than a metaphysical principle) who experiences the world, responds to what happens, relates to us and interacts dynamically with humans.[1]

Pinnock endorses the second model and identifies it as open theism.[2] But this description of supposedly common models of God doesn't quite ring true. My impression is that most Christians combine elements of both models: God is a monarch, but not aloof. He is an all-determining and irresistible power, but also a caring parent.[3] He is not contingent (that is, dependent) on the world, but neither is he "removed from the contingencies of the world," for he is very much involved in the world he has made. He is aware of everything that happens and never takes risks, yet he abounds in love and responsiveness, generosity and sensitivity. He is a person, not merely a metaphysical principle.[4] Nor do I think that most Christians (even

1. Clark H. Pinnock, "Systematic Theology," in *The Openness of God,* by Clark H. Pinnock, Richard Rice, John Sanders, William Hasker, and David Basinger (Downers Grove, Ill.: InterVarsity Press, 1994) (henceforth cited as OG), 103.

2. I should note that Pinnock intends the first model to represent "the God of Greek philosophy," rather than the God of traditional Christian theism, but he does regard the two as largely equivalent. I wonder, incidentally, which Greek philosophers he has in mind. See the section on "God and the Greeks" in chapter 2.

3. God is not only a parent, but a father (*pace* feminism)! He is, indeed, "our Father in heaven," as Jesus taught us to address him (Matt. 6:9). But Scripture relates our Father's heavenly domain to his irresistible power: "Are you not the God who is in heaven? You rule over all the kingdoms of the nations. Power and might are in your hand, and no one can withstand you" (2 Chron. 20:6).

4. He is both a person and a metaphysical principle, the very cornerstone of the universe. That is to say, he is both absolute and personal. For more discussion of God's remarkable combination of absoluteness and personality, see my *Cornelius Van Til* (Phillipsburg, N.J.: P&R Publishing, 1995), 51–61.

traditional ones) would object to Pinnock's description of God as one "who experiences the world, responds to what happens, relates to us and interacts dynamically with humans."[5]

What Pinnock presents as two distinct models of God are, for the most part, aspects of a single model—the biblical model that has governed the thinking of most Christians through the centuries. I would reject two elements in the first list (God's aloofness and his removal from the world process), and I would question two from the second list (God's openness and his vulnerability).[6] I think most Christians throughout history would agree with me.

1ST objection

The Openness of the Sovereign God

I said that I question Pinnock's terms *openness* and *vulnerability,* not that I reject them. In fact, I can affirm these terms in some senses. However, they are ambiguous. *Openness* is, of course, a metaphor. It is not used in Scripture as an attribute of God, and it does not have a standard meaning in the theological literature. Richard Rice defines it as showing that open theism "regards God as receptive to new experiences and as flexible in the way he works toward his objectives in the world."[7]

But I believe that Pinnock and others use the word *open* also because of its connotations.[8] The term has a good feel

---

5. Open theists, of course, question whether these qualities can be integrated into the traditional view of God. I shall argue in this book that they can be.

6. This is a kind of rhetorical trick, concealing potentially controversial assertions in an uncontroversial context. Pinnock here evidently expects the favorable connotations of *love, responsiveness, generosity, sensitivity,* etc., to rub off on *openness* and *vulnerability.* Open theists speak this way rather often, and it does not serve the cause of clarity or edification.

7. Richard Rice, "Biblical Support for a New Perspective," in OG, 16.

8. The phrase *open theism* seems to have been used first by Rice in *The Openness of God: The Relationship of Divine Foreknowledge and Human Free Will* (Washington: Review and Herald, 1980). The book was republished as *God's Foreknowledge and Man's Free Will* (Minneapolis: Bethany House, 1985).

---

to it. It suggests vistas of spacious meadows, full of merry sunshine, welcome mats, unlocked gates, undogmatic thinking, and people who are willing to share their inmost secrets. That kind of imagery is certainly attractive to people in our culture. But we should be careful of it. Sometimes, after all, closed is better than open. Food will spoil if we leave the refrigerator door open. An open safe is an invitation to thieves. And it is not wise to leave the door of a moving car open. Perhaps it is better, in some respects, for God to be closed. For example, if he really has left the future completely open, he has left open the possibility of Satan's victory.

The sovereign God of traditional Christian theism is closed in certain ways, as we shall see. But in other respects he is also a God of openness. He opens the world wonderfully to his children, commanding them to exercise dominion over the whole earth (Gen. 1:28), enabling Paul to say that he can do all things through Christ (Phil. 4:13)! He sets an open door before his people as they proclaim Christ throughout the world (Col. 4:3; Rev. 3:8). God can open and close the doors of creation precisely because he is sovereign: "What he opens no one can shut, and what he shuts no one can open" (Rev. 3:7).

His sovereignty makes him fully open to our prayers, for he is always able to answer them. No door is closed to him. He can, indeed, even open the doors of human hearts to his influence; we cannot keep him out. His sovereign power opens us to him and him to us.

So the openness metaphor cuts both ways. Indeed, the relatively few biblical uses of *open* fit better with the traditional model than with Pinnock's. But, of course, theology should not be built on metaphors, which typically can be taken in many different directions, but rather on the teaching of Scripture.

Sovereign Vulnerability

Vulnerability is an idea that I shall discuss later in this book. My own view is that God cannot suffer loss in his essential nature, and that his eternal plan cannot suffer any defeat. In those senses, he is invulnerable. But when he interacts with creatures, yes, he does experience grief (Eph. 4:30). Jesus was vulnerable unto death, and he is nothing less than God the Son. And even apart from the Incarnation, the prophet declares that "in all their distress [God] too was distressed" (Isa. 63:9). This biblical emphasis is fully compatible with classical theism, as I shall argue in this book.[9]

The Ambiguities of Open Theism

We have not, however, made much progress in defining the nature of open theism and its precise differences with the traditional view. Pinnock's two lists, as we have seen, are far too vague, ambiguous, and misleading to define the differences. I have spent some time on his lists in order to show that the appeal of open theism is often based on connotations, on the sounds of words, on rhetoric, rather than substance.

Another example is provided by the preface to *The Openness of God:*

> God, in grace, grants humans significant freedom to cooperate with or work against God's will for their lives, and he enters into dynamic, give-and-take relationships with us.

9. Alister E. McGrath refers to Luther's theology of the cross and Charles Wesley's hymn "And Can It Be" as examples of traditional theologians affirming in various ways the vulnerability of God. He comments about OG: "Why should we abandon this tradition when, in fact, it has not been fairly and thoroughly presented in this book? Modern evangelicalism has often been accused of a lack of familiarity with its own historical roots and traditions. Curiously, this book merely confirms that impression" ("Whatever Happened to Luther?" *Christianity Today,* January 9, 1995, 34).

The Christian life involves a genuine interaction between God and human beings. We respond to God's gracious initiatives and God responds to our responses . . . and on it goes. God takes risks in this give-and-take relationship, yet he is endlessly resourceful and competent in working toward his ultimate goals. Sometimes God alone decides how to accomplish these goals. On other occasions, God works with human decisions, adapting his own plans to fit the changing situation. God does not control everything that happens. Rather, he is open to receiving input from his creatures. In loving dialogue, God invites us to participate with him to bring the future into being.[10]

The authors admit, to their credit, that this description of open theism is only in "broad strokes."[11] But this is the sort of description that grabs the attention and emotions of the average reader. The authors offer to take us on a grand adventure, with great risk, but arm in arm with God himself. Who would not want to come along?

But what is "significant freedom"? Open theists also describe it as "real freedom" or "genuine freedom." (Compare the later reference to "a genuine interaction.") Of course, everybody wants to have "genuine" freedom, and everybody would like to believe he has it. (Indeed, what other kind of freedom is there?) But that language hugely prejudices the discussion. As we shall see below, open theism teaches a particular view of freedom, namely, libertarianism, which is highly controversial in theology. I shall argue that the concept is unbiblical and incoherent. And, upon careful analysis, it turns out not to be genuine freedom at all, but a kind of bondage to unpredictable chance.

And what is a "dynamic" relationship to God, as opposed to a static one? Modern theology praises things that are dynamic and demonizes anything static, and the authors of *The*

10. Preface to OG, 7.
11. Ibid.

No Other God

Openness of God follow that trend dutifully. But what, actually, is the difference? Evidently, in this context, *dynamic* means "changing," rather than "powerful." But even in classical theology, our relationship to God changes in some respects, even though God in himself does not change. That is, God is unchanging in his nature and eternal plan, but his relationships with creatures do change. So in fact both classical theology and open theism promise us a dynamic relationship with God.

And do we really want to exclude all static (unchanging) aspects of our relationship to God? Is it not important that some aspects of that relationship do not change, such as God's promises, his way of salvation, and his justice, holiness, and mercy? Does not the writer of Psalm 136 delight in repeating the refrain, "His love endures forever"? Would any open theist be pleased to see God's love change to cruelty?

I plead with readers of open-theist writings not to be carried away with rhetoric. Don't let anything get past you. Think it through; ask what these writers really mean. Don't let them sweep you off your feet by means of ambiguous, but rhetorically attractive, language.

The Open-Theist View of Traditional Theism

We must now move from the rhetorical to the real differences between open and traditional theism. Open theists, to their credit, do sometimes move beyond the rhetorical posture to an analytical one. Richard Rice, for example, gives us a rather precise account of the issues, and we should look at that. We should consider first the open theists' view of what traditional theism teaches. Here is my summary of what Rice calls the "traditional" or "conventional" view:[12]

12. Rice, "Biblical Support," in OG, 11–12. John Sanders, in "Historical Considerations," in OG, 59, calls the traditional view "the classical view of God worked out in the Western tradition."

1. It emphasizes God's sovereignty, majesty, and glory.
2. God's will is the final explanation of everything.
3. His will is irresistible.
4. He is caring and benevolent, but he is glorified equally in the destruction of the wicked.
5. He is supratemporal.
6. He knows everything in the past, present, and future.
7. He is essentially unaffected by human events and experiences.

The terms *traditional* and *conventional* suggest that most theological traditions would agree with these propositions. But, in fact, Rice's description reflects Calvinist beliefs specifically, more than any other tradition. Arminians, for example, would not agree that God's will is the final explanation of everything or that his will is irresistible. On the other hand, not all Calvinists would agree that God is glorified equally (or in every sense) in the salvation of the righteous and the destruction of the wicked. Calvinists believe that God equally foreordains both of these outcomes, as he foreordains all the events of nature and history. But not all events are pleasing to him, and in that sense all events do not equally glorify him. As for the destruction of the wicked, Scripture says that God takes no delight in that (Ezek. 33:11), and many Calvinists take that teaching quite literally.[13] Nevertheless, Rice's list indicates the views that open theists want to reject.

13. Calvinists distinguish between God's "decretive" and "preceptive" wills. The former is God's eternal decree, which necessarily comes to pass; the latter is God's standard of behavior. No one can violate God's will in the first sense, but many violate it in the second sense. In the first sense, everything that happens brings glory to God; in the second sense, he is glorified only by the obedience of his creatures. See my discussion of this distinction in chapter 7.

The Main Contentions of Open Theism

Later, Rice sets forth his own view of God, which he shares with other open theists. Again, I paraphrase and summarize, using much of Rice's own language:[14]

[handwritten margin note: Open Theist views most opposed]

1. Love is God's most important quality.
2. Love is not only care and commitment, but also being sensitive and responsive.
3. Creatures exert an influence on God.
4. God's will is not the ultimate explanation of everything. History is the combined result of what God and his creatures decide to do.
5. God does not know everything timelessly, but learns from events as they take place.
6. So God is dependent on the world in some ways.

There is also a seventh proposition that Rice does not mention here, but which is central to open theism—possibly even the root from which the whole system grows:

7. Human beings are free in the libertarian sense.

Libertarianism is the philosophical name for what Pinnock calls "significant freedom" in a passage I quoted earlier. The open-theist philosopher William Hasker defines libertarian free will as follows:

> An agent is free with respect to a given action at a given time if at that time it is within the agent's power to perform the action and also in the agent's power to refrain from the action.[15]

---

14. Rice, "Biblical Support," in OG, 15–16.
15. William Hasker, "A Philosophical Perspective," in OG, 136–37.

On this view, our free choices are absolutely undetermined and uncaused. They are not foreordained by God, or by circumstances, or even by our own character or desires. I shall argue in chapter 8 that this view of freedom is unscriptural. Scripture does affirm that we are free to act according to our desires and nature, and that God's grace can set us free from sin to serve Christ. However, it does not teach libertarianism, but rather excludes it. Further, I shall argue that, contrary to Hasker and others, libertarianism does not establish moral responsibility, but rather destroys it.

In the chapters that follow, I shall examine these distinctive contentions of open theism, both positive and negative, by comparing them with the teaching of the Bible.

Where Does Open Theism Come From?

The focus of this book is mostly analytical and evaluative, rather than historical. Nevertheless, to understand a theological movement, it is important to know something of its history. This is especially the case in regard to open theism, for its advocates often represent the movement as something very contemporary. For them, the newness of open theism is a major reason why people should be attracted to it. Pinnock, for example, presents the "classical" view of God as "a being which is immutable and impassible," and then comments a little later:

> For most of us today, however, this immobility of God is by no means attractive. We are not thrilled to learn that God is self-enclosed reality and utterly changeless.[1]

Still later, he says:

> I admit that modern culture has influenced me in this matter. The new emphasis upon human freedom requires that

1. Clark Pinnock, "Between Classical and Process Theism," in *Process Theology,* ed. Ronald H. Nash (Grand Rapids: Baker, 1987), 315.

I think of God as self-limited in relation to the world. For the Greeks it may have been natural to place God completely beyond the temporal flow, in a serene magisterial aloofness. But for us it certainly is not. . . . The modern world invites us to restore the positive assessment of history and change and in so doing draw closer to biblical teaching. Let no one say that modernity always lures us away and never beckons us toward the truth.[2]

John Sanders's chapter on "Historical Considerations" in *The Openness of God*[3] presents a similar picture: Traditional theism is a mixture of Greek philosophy and biblical teaching, which has dominated the thinking of the Christian church up to the twentieth century. But "modern theology has witnessed a remarkable reexamination of the nature and attributes of God."[4] Indeed, theology is going through a "paradigm shift," according to Roger Olson.[5] So open theism is a contemporary option, something quite new, a "new model" of God.

This emphasis on newness is a large part of the appeal of open theism. Pinnock wants a theology that is "attractive" to people today, rather than bogged down in the past. There are many dangers in this approach, of course. Christians should be the first to deny that the newest is the truest.[6] And much of what is "attractive to people today" is by no means Christian.

However, open theists do seek to justify their position from Scripture as well, so I don't want to press this point too heavily. But I would like to call into question the open theists'

2. Ibid., 317.
3. Pp. 59–100.
4. John Sanders, "Historical Considerations," in OG, 91.
5. Roger Olson, "Has God Been Held Hostage by Philosophy?" *Christianity Today,* January 9, 1995, 30.
6. To claim that the newness of an idea makes it more likely to be true is an instance of the genetic fallacy. Traditionalism (which reveres ideas because of their antiquity) and modernism (which embraces ideas because of their newness) are equally fallacious. Protestant Christians renounce both of these in favor of the principle of *sola Scriptura,* which judges theological ideas by their agreement with Scripture.

NO OTHER GOD

claim to newness. Inquirers, especially those who are attracted to newness, need to understand that open theism is not as new as it claims to be. Indeed, in some respects the open theists would be better advised to advertise their position on the ground of its antiquity, rather than its contemporaneity.

This chapter will not be an original work of historiography. I will be very brief and cite mainly secondary sources, including the writings of the open theists themselves. A thorough historical study of the roots of open theism, however useful, would require far more than a chapter, and it would detract from the main argument of the book, which is exegetical. As I have argued elsewhere, although historical studies have their value, they can never resolve any theological issue. Only Scripture (*sola Scriptura*) can judge between theological alternatives.[7] Further, my purpose here is simply to note some fairly obvious correlations between open theism and past intellectual movements. I cite secondary sources intentionally, as Cornelius Van Til often did, to show that my understanding of the history is not idiosyncratic.

The Antiquity of Open Theism

Sanders himself admits that one crucial, distinctive element (*the* crucial element, in my view) of open theism, is ancient: libertarian free will. He notes that that concept can be found in Philo[8] and in a number of the early church fathers.[9] He

---

7. See my "In Defense of Something Close to Biblicism," *Westminster Theological Journal* 59 (1997), 268–318, also published as *"Sola Scriptura* in Theological Method," in *Contemporary Worship Music: A Biblical Defense* (Phillipsburg, N.J.: P&R Publishing, 1997), 175–201, and my "Traditionalism," available at www.thirdmill.org.

8. Sanders, "Historical Considerations," 71.

9. Sanders refers to Justin Martyr (ibid., 73), Irenaeus (p. 74), Tertullian (p. 74), Origen (p. 75), and the early Augustine (p. 81). (He points out that Augustine later turned away from libertarianism.)

---

finds libertarianism also, of course, in the writings of Jacob Arminius (d. 1609), the opponent of Calvinism.[10] So evidently libertarianism is not a new idea.

Historians of philosophy would add that the idea goes back even further, to the Greek philosopher Epicurus (341–270 B.C.). He believed that the world was made of tiny atoms that normally move downward in vertical lines. But if these atoms are to collide, combine, and produce larger objects, they must occasionally swerve from the vertical. This swerving is unpredictable and random. For Epicurus, swerving explains the formation of objects and also the nature of human freedom and responsibility.[11]

Plato (427–347 B.C.) and Aristotle (384–322 B.C.) also held to a kind of randomness in nature, the realm of the sense-world (Plato) or of prime matter (Aristotle). These realms are radically indeterminate, because they are not "forms" or "ideas."[12]

Consistent with this conception, the gods of Plato and Aristotle are far from the sovereign God of Scripture. Plato refers to a number of beings as divine: (1) The gods of the Greek religions, who are finite. (2) The Demiurge of the *Timaeus,* who forms the material "receptacle" into a copy of

10. Ibid., 91.
11. My main critique of libertarianism will come later, in chapter 8. But I can't resist pointing out here how inadequate Epicurus's libertarianism is as an account of moral responsibility. Is it even conceivable that my moral responsibility is based on the chance movements of atoms swerving around in my body? This view turns our moral decisions into accidents, random events. Would anyone consider me to be responsible for these chance events? Accidental physical events in the body (like the catching of viruses that impede mental concentration) would seem to mitigate responsibility, rather than create it.
12. Forms or ideas are the qualities or properties of objects: shape, size, color, value, virtue, etc. For Plato, objects in this world are copies of Forms that exist in a higher world. For Aristotle, forms are found in and with things in the world of our experience. On both views, forms somehow get attached to, or associated with, material objects. The matter *bears* the form. But the matter beneath the form, the unformed matter, lacks form and therefore lacks structure.

NO OTHER GOD

the world of Forms. The Demiurge is constrained both by the nature of the Forms and by the nature of the material. (3) The world of Forms itself, especially the Form of the Good. But for Plato, the Form of the Good explains only the goodness of the world, not its defects or evils. So all the beings Plato refers to as gods are essentially finite. They do not control the world, but rather are themselves limited by the world's autonomy, by chance, by (in effect) the libertarian freedom of finite beings.

Aristotle's god is his "Prime Mover," the one who moves all things, but is not himself moved. This being is impersonal, rather than personal. As open theists often note, Aristotle's god does not know the world or love the world. He moves the world by attracting finite beings to move themselves in his direction, as a beautiful piece of art attracts visitors to a gallery. This view is essentially a libertarian concept of divine causation. To use language that is common in process theology, Aristotle's god moves the world "persuasively" rather than "coercively."[13]

The premises underlying libertarianism go back even further. The earliest Greek philosophers, such as Thales, Anaximander, and Anaximenes, sought to explain the world order and process without reference to gods. So their worldview did not allow for a personal being who controls the world by an eternal plan. The world functions on its own, autonomously, and the philosopher comes to understand that world autonomously, using reason apart from divine revelation. It is not always clear whether these thinkers conceived of the world process deterministically or indeterministically,

---

13. *Persuasion* is itself somewhat inappropriate as a description of the Prime Mover's influence on the world. For Aristotle's god is impersonal, as unable to persuade as he is to coerce. Aristotle's god is even more passive than the deity of open theism. But this god certainly has more in common with open theism than with traditional theism.

but their thinking avoids the most obvious barrier to libertarianism, namely, the notion of a sovereign, personal God.

I should note in passing that the above comments offer a partial reply to the complaint of open theists that traditional theism is partially based on Greek philosophy. We shall consider this question in other contexts, but we can already see that, so far as libertarian freedom is concerned, open theism is more Greek than is traditional theism.

We can trace this development even further back in time—indeed, to the beginning of history. Belief in human autonomy, the root of libertarianism, goes back to the fall of man. As recorded in Genesis 3, Adam and Eve came to believe that they could stand in a neutral position between God and Satan and autonomously decide which supernatural being was telling the truth. Implicitly, they came to believe, if only for a tragic moment, Satan's lie: that God was not in control of the world he had made.

My point is that non-Christian thought, throughout its history, has been implicitly libertarian. It is true that many non-Christian thinkers whom I have not mentioned, such as the Stoics, Spinoza, and B. F. Skinner, have been determinists, and that determinism (the view that every event is completely explainable by previous efficient causes) seems contrary to libertarianism. But from a Calvinistic perspective, secular determinism is a close cousin to libertarianism, for neither acknowledges that the world is under the control of a personal creator. In both systems, therefore, the world process "just happens." In both, the ruling element is chance.

The same may be said of Neoplatonism and the other Hellenistic philosophies that Roger Olson particularly connects with traditional theism.[14] Neoplatonism taught the existence of an impersonal supreme being who, although oppo-

14. Olson, "Has God Been Held Hostage by Philosophy?" 30.

site in some ways to the irrational flux of the material world, was correlative to it, being unable to prevent its imperfections.

Open theism, therefore, draws on some ideas that have been in the world since Eden. I do not wish to equate open theism with ancient idolatry or with secular forms of libertarianism, but open-theist libertarianism shares many concepts with them. To say this is not to prove that those concepts are wrong. But these conceptual parallels refute the notion that open theism is uniquely contemporary, an utterly fresh insight. We have also seen that people holding these ideas have not always held them out of a desire to be faithful to Scripture.

God and the Greeks

Another conclusion that follows from the above discussion is that open theism owes at least as much to Greek philosophy as classical theism does. Open theists have often argued that classical theism is in effect a combination of biblical teaching and Greek philosophy. I don't deny that some Greek philosophical concepts of divine unchangeability, impassibility, etc., have influenced classical theism, although we must yet discuss whether this influence was good or bad. But open theism also has affinities with Greek thought, as we have seen. Its view of libertarian freedom was held by some Greek philosophers and was implicit in the teachings of others.

The open theists' comparisons between Greek philosophy and classical theism are not always convincing. Recall Pinnock's statement that I quoted in chapter 1:

> We may think of God primarily as an aloof monarch, removed from the contingencies of the world, unchangeable in every aspect of being, as an all-determining and irresistible power, aware of everything that will ever happen and never taking risks. Or we may understand God as a car-

ing parent with qualities of love and responsiveness, generosity and sensitivity, openness and vulnerability, a person (rather than a metaphysical principle) who experiences the world, responds to what happens, relates to us and interacts dynamically with humans.[15]

Here Pinnock contrasts what he considers to be the Greek philosophical view of God with his open view. He seems to think that classical theology is closer to the Greek view. But I wonder which Greek philosophers he has in mind here. No Greek philosopher, to my knowledge, thought of God as a monarch. In most Greek philosophical systems, God was impersonal, and monarchs are, of course, personal. Greek religion included personal gods, one of which, Zeus, was monarchical in a sense, but these gods were certainly not "aloof," "unchangeable," "irresistible," etc. Plato's Demiurge was not "all-determining," and his divine Good caused only good things, not evil. Aristotle's impersonal Prime Mover was not aware of anything that took place in the finite world—not "aware of everything." The Stoic deity approached Pinnock's characterization, but was pantheistic or panentheistic.

Neither open theism nor classical theism should be disparaged merely because of the historical movements that have influenced it. But when we make comparisons between contemporary movements and historical ones, we should seek to make those comparisons more carefully than Pinnock does.

Socinianism: the Missing Link in Open Theism's Genealogy

Besides libertarianism, another central idea of open theism is also rather old: its denial of God's exhaustive foreknowledge. That denial also has an important historical precedent.

15. Clark H. Pinnock, "Systematic Theology," in OG, 103.

After discussing Arminius in his historical survey, Sanders jumps to the twentieth century and talks about Paul Tillich and others. But he thereby leaves out a movement that is important to the history of open-theist ideas: Socinianism. The Italians Lelio Socinus (1525–62) and his nephew Fausto Socinus (1539–1604) were regarded as heretical by both Protestants and Catholics. They denied the full deity of Christ, his substitutionary atonement, and justification by the imputed righteousness of Christ. Robert Strimple notes these views and then adds:

> But Socinianism also held to a heretical doctrine of God. The Socinian doctrine can be stated very briefly, and it must be contrasted with both Calvinism and Arminianism. Calvinism (or Augustinianism) teaches that the sovereign God has *foreordained* whatsoever comes to pass, and therefore He *foreknows* whatsoever comes to pass. Arminianism denies that God has foreordained whatsoever comes to pass but wishes nevertheless to affirm God's foreknowledge of whatsoever comes to pass. Against the Arminians, the Socinians insisted that logically the Calvinists were quite correct in insisting that the only real basis for believing that God *knows* what you are going to do next is to believe that he has *foreordained* what you are going to do next. How else could God know ahead of time what your decision will be? Like the Arminians, however, the Socinians insisted that it was a contradiction of human freedom to believe in the sovereign foreordination of God. So they went "all the way" (logically) and denied not only that God has foreordained the free decisions of free agents but also that God foreknows what those decisions will be.
>
> That is precisely the teaching of the "free will theism" of Pinnock, Rice, and other like-minded "new model evangelicals." They want their doctrine of God to sound very "new," very modern, by dressing it up with references to Heisenberg's uncertainty principle in physics and to the insights of process theology (although they reject process the-

ology as a whole . . .). But it is just the old Socinian heresy
rejected by the church centuries ago.[16]

Strimple adds that the parallel between Socinianism and
open theism extends even to their "most basic arguments."
Open theists argue that *omniscience* means knowing all that is
knowable, and since the free decisions of creatures are not
knowable, ignorance of them does not count against God's
omniscience. Strimple points out that this is "a direct echo of
the Socinian argument."[17]

It is remarkable that none of the open theists refer to
Socinianism as a root of their doctrine. Sanders skips over it
in his historical survey, as does Pinnock in the account of his
theological pilgrimage.[18] But their view of God's knowledge
is clearly Socinian. My point is not to charge the open theists
with all the heresies of Socinianism, or even to imply that they
have been concealing something about their heritage. Perhaps
they have been unaware of the Socinian connection, although
such ignorance would not reflect well on the quality of their
historical scholarship.[19] I merely wish to point out that their
position is not new at all, and that it has been part of a system, the main tenets of which most Christians throughout
history (including the open theists) would disavow.

Why is this important? Strimple comments that it helps us
to guard against the false notion

16. Robert B. Strimple, "What Does God Know?" in *The Coming Evangelical
Crisis,* ed. John H. Armstrong (Chicago: Moody Press, 1996), 140–41.
17. Ibid., 141.
18. Clark H. Pinnock, "From Augustine to Arminius," in *The Grace of God
and the Will of Man,* ed. Clark H. Pinnock (Grand Rapids: Zondervan, 1989),
15–30.
19. I will not comment in general on the quality of open-theist historiography, but I should note that some critics of open theism have taken the movement to task for its inadequate understanding of the theological tradition. See
Douglas F. Kelly, "Afraid of Infinitude," and Alister E. McGrath, "Whatever
Happened to Luther?" in the forum "Has God Been Held Hostage by
Philosophy?" *Christianity Today,* January 9, 1995, 30–34.

No Other God

that perhaps if our Reformation forefathers had only known these ideas they would have rethought their doctrine of God. Quite the contrary, our Reformation forefathers were presented with the modern Rice/Pinnock arguments in the form of Socinianism and clearly rejected them. Lelio Socinus pestered Calvin and Melanchthon with letter after letter in which he set forth such views, and the Reformers rejected Socinus's views as untrue to the biblical witness.[20]

And we who, like the Reformers, believe that God knows the future exhaustively can trace the denial of that doctrine even further back in history than the time of the Socinians. We think of the scoffers in Psalm 73:11 who say, "How can God know? Does the Most High have knowledge?" And we recall the idolaters of Isaiah's day, who ignored the fact that the true God demonstrates his deity against the false gods by declaring "the things to come" (Isa. 41:22; cf. vv. 21–29). Just as unbelief gravitates toward libertarianism, as we saw in the last section, so it tends to deny God's knowledge of the future. The reason is the same in both cases. Unbelievers want to live autonomously, and a God who controls the world and knows the future is a barrier to that autonomy.

Again, I am not charging open theists with all the errors of their predecessors, whether the Socinians or the idolaters of Isaiah's time. Nor are the open theists wrong merely because of the historical background of their positions. Rather, the point of this discussion is that the central positions of open theism are ancient, rather than contemporary. And we should be cautious in examining the ideas of open

---

20. Strimple, "What Does God Know?" 141. He cites Thomas M. Lindsay, *A History of the Reformation* (New York: Scribner's, 1938), 2:471.

---

theism, since they have sometimes appeared in the service of unbelief.

More Recent Influences

However, we should also take seriously the testimony of open theists that they have been largely influenced by contemporary movements and issues. As Pinnock says in the passage quoted earlier, one influence upon him has been "modern culture," including "the new emphasis upon human freedom." (The emphasis may be new, but the idea certainly is not.)

But there is in Pinnock's account an unhealthy reverence for what is recent. Note his statement that the modern emphasis "requires that I think of God as self-limited in relation to the world." *Requires?* He seems to be saying that modern culture constrains him—and all Christians, by implication— to change their theology. What a horrible idea! Christians should reject such a notion in the strongest terms. Only God in his Word has the right to tell Christians what they must believe, and Christians should be willing to defend the teachings of God's Word against any and all intellectual fashions.

A somewhat more sympathetic reading of Pinnock here might be to take him as saying that the modern emphasis on human freedom has led him to a better way of reading the Bible, and that his new exegesis, in turn, requires him to think of God as self-limited. Certainly it is not wrong for us to reread the Bible in response to cultural challenges, to see if we have perhaps been reading it wrongly. But Pinnock does seem to be saying that modern culture requires a certain exegesis of Scripture, and that should never be.

Open theism is not the first intellectual movement to revise classical theism in response to the modern emphasis on freedom. That emphasis has influenced a number of philosophers and theologians since the eighteenth century who have sought to limit divine sovereignty to make more room for human free choice. David Hume suggested in his *Dialogues Concerning Natural Religion* that a finite god might be sufficient to meet the needs of faith.[21] John Stuart Mill agreed.[22] Immanuel Kant removed God from the realm of human experience, in part to make room for libertarian freedom. German and British Idealists taught that the absolute being is correlative to the world of space and time—that is, that God and the world are mutually dependent.[23] William James (1842–1910) taught the existence of a finite god who struggles with us to combat evil. For him, God must be finite if we are to be free, and James identified freedom with "chance."[24] In the early twentieth century, the school of Boston Personalism (Borden P. Bowne, Edgar S. Brightman, Albert C. Knudson, Peter Bertocci) insisted that God was finite and correlative to human libertarian freedom. Others who made similar arguments were John Fiske, Henri Bergson, Andrew Seth Pringle-Pattison, F. H. Bradley, and H. G. Wells.[25]

21. E. A. Burtt, ed., *The English Philosophers from Bacon to Mill* (New York: Modern Library, n.d.), 741.

22. John Stuart Mill, *Three Essays on Religion* (New York: Greenword Press, 1969), 130–31.

23. See, for example, Cornelius Van Til, *Christianity and Idealism* (Philadelphia: Presbyterian and Reformed, 1955). Many philosophical systems have argued for a correlativity between God and the world: e.g., Gnosticism, Neoplatonism, and the system of Spinoza.

24. William James, *The Will to Believe* (New York: Dowen Publications, n.d.), 180.

25. There is a useful survey of these and other figures in Robert A. Morey, *Battle of the Gods* (Southbridge, Mass.: Crown Publications, 1989), 69–102. Note also some (somewhat more obscure) antecedents of open theism in Gregory A. Boyd, *God of the Possible* (Grand Rapids: Baker, 2000), 115. Boyd is wrong to include in his list the Bible commentator Adam Clarke. Roger Nicole, in "A Review Article: God of the Possible?" *Reformation and Revival* 10, no. 1 (winter 2001), 192, shows that Clarke's handling of Num. 23:19, Jer. 18, Jonah 3:10, and James 1:17 is very different from that of open theism. Clarke denies that God ever changes his mind, and he denies that God is "affected by the changes and chances to which mortal things are exposed."

Academic theologians in the twentieth century have often taken a similar line, emphasizing human freedom and divine vulnerability. Sanders takes note of Jürgen Moltmann and Wolfhart Pannenberg, for whom "Jesus reveals that God is involved in history and is willing to become vulnerable."[26] He also mentions Emil Brunner, Hendrikus Berkhof, Eberhard Jüngel, Colin Gunton, the Roman Catholic feminists Catherine LaCugna and Elizabeth Johnson, and others who have affinity with open theism.

For most of the twentieth century, however, the most influential movement stressing libertarian freedom and divine vulnerability has been the process philosophy of Samuel Alexander, Alfred North Whitehead, and Charles Hartshorne, together with the process theology of such thinkers as John Cobb, Schubert Ogden, and David Ray Griffin. Open theists commend process theology for its critique of classical theism, but they also take exception to some distinctive teachings of process thought, such as its lack of a doctrine of creation, its insistence that God always works persuasively rather than coercively, its view that all of God's actions are dependent on the world, and its lack of assurance that God's purposes will triumph in the end.[27]

What Is New About Open Theism?

The ideas of open theism are not new, therefore, nor have the open theists been particularly creative in rethinking the older perspectives. Their ideas are largely ancient, and many have held similar views in the past century. Open theism is distinctive mainly as a theological movement. It has brought together a group of writers who are more or less of one mind

26. Sanders, "Historical Considerations," 98.
27. William Hasker, "A Philosophical Perspective," in OG, 138–41; Pinnock, "Between Classical and Process Theism," 317–20.

on these matters, with the definite intention of persuading the church to go their way. The open theists have authored and coauthored a number of books that many have found persuasive. They have presented their ideas vividly, with passion and excitement. The appeal of open theism, in other words, is in its presentation, rather than in the freshness of its ideas.

Open theism is also distinctive in that it has been an "evangelical" movement. The term *evangelical* has been traditionally used to describe Protestants who believe in the inerrancy of Scripture and in justification by grace through faith in the finished work of Christ. Evangelicals have also been known for their belief in biblical supernaturalism, including the virgin birth of Jesus, his miracles, his substitutionary atonement, and his resurrection. But today, the label "evangelical" is attached to many who reject biblical inerrancy, which makes it difficult to define in the present context. The open theists claim to be evangelicals, but they reject doctrines (such as God's exhaustive foreknowledge) that have never before been controversial in evangelical circles.

The libertarian view of freedom has, of course, long existed in the Arminian strand of the evangelical tradition. Open theists often identify themselves specifically as Arminians (although, as we have seen, they are more Socinian on this matter). But they believe that traditional Arminianism has not been consistent enough with its view of libertarian freedom. In traditional Arminianism, although God does not predetermine man's free choices, he does know them all in advance, for he knows the future exhaustively. The open theists ask, quite properly, how God can foreknow human free choices without foreordaining them. If human free choices are knowable in advance, they must somehow be settled in advance. And that is what libertarianism denies. Open theists, then, agree with Calvinists that divine foreknowledge entails divine foreordination, and therefore that traditional Arminianism is inadequate. But rather than accept the Calvinist doctrine of foreordination, they reject both divine foreordination and divine foreknowledge.[28]

The main question before us, therefore, is not whether open theism is fresh, or new, or otherwise appealing, or whether it is true to its evangelical heritage. The issue, rather, is whether it is biblical. This question will occupy our attention for the remainder of this book.

As a Calvinist, I reject both traditional Arminianism and open theism. Of the two, the former is more biblical in my judgment, the latter more logically consistent. Certainly Arminianism is better, since it is better to be inconsistently scriptural than to achieve consistency with an error. But it is evident that we can be satisfied with neither position.

28. For a more thorough account of the relationship between open theism and traditional Arminianism, see Bruce A. Ware's chapter on "The Perceived Inadequacy of the Classical Arminian View of God," in *God's Lesser Glory* (Wheaton, Ill.: Crossway Books, 2000), 31–42.

T H R E E

How Do Open Theists Read the Bible?

Before examining the substantive issues raised by open theism, I should discuss the methods used by open theists to reach their conclusions. In general, as we have seen, open theists focus on the Bible. This focus distinguishes them somewhat from many philosophers and theologians (some of whom are listed in the preceding chapter) who hold similar views. The open theists believe and seek to demonstrate, above all, that their position is more biblical than traditional theism. To evaluate this claim, we must give some attention to their method of interpreting the Bible.

No theology simply repeats the words of the Bible. Theology uses extrascriptural words and phrases, and schemes of organization other than the Bible's own. Evangelical theologians, nevertheless, claim that their writings are faithful to Scripture. They maintain that their theological works help readers to understand the Bible, that is, to apply it to their thoughts and lives.[1]

---

1. For an extended account of theology as application, see my *The Doctrine of the Knowledge of God* (Phillipsburg, N.J.: Presbyterian and Reformed, 1987).

So, although we must admit the extrabiblical influences on our theological formulations, we should not allow those influences to determine what we say. Our goal should be to let Scripture speak its own message. Only God's Word stands as the supreme authority for theology and for all of life. Other sources of knowledge may inform theology, but they should not constrain it.

There are, however, a number of extrabiblical factors that determine open-theist exegesis. We have already seen that "the new emphasis upon human freedom" places an unseemly constraint upon Pinnock's exegesis of Scripture. And we shall see (especially in chapter 8) that the doctrine of human freedom in the libertarian sense serves as a nonnegotiable presupposition. Open theists insist on interpreting all biblical teachings in a manner that is consistent with libertarianism, without seriously submitting libertarianism itself to a biblical critique. For now, however, I will focus my attention on two other exegetical constraints in open theism.

Logic

All theologians seek to be logical. But, as logic books themselves inform us, there are right and wrong ways to use logic. The laws of logic are universally and necessarily valid, but our use of them, like our use of everything else, is fallible, because of our finitude and sin. In God's mind, there are no contradictions. But human arguments err in many ways, and human systems of logic are not infallible, either.[2]

Sanders rejects "the appeal to antinomies," which he understands as the view that certain teachings of Scripture are

2. For an extended treatment of the use of logic in theology, see ibid., 242–301, and also my *Cornelius Van Til* (Phillipsburg, N.J.: P&R Publishing, 1995), 151–75. An article that concisely and helpfully sets forth the powers and limits of logic is Richard Pratt, "Does God Observe the Law of Contradiction? . . . Should We?" available at www.thirdmill.org.

apparently contradictory. He recognizes that his opponents, the traditional theists, themselves reject the possibility of *real* contradiction in the Bible. And in fact he defends the consistency of traditional theism in relating divine sovereignty to human freedom. He recognizes that traditionalists hold a definition of freedom that is different from his libertarianism,[3] one that is consistent with their view of divine sovereignty.[4] At the same time, however, he believes that traditional theists make an illegitimate "appeal to antinomies," that they appeal to "apparent contradictions."[5]

Sanders accuses traditional theists of holding that "certain doctrines are genuine contradictions for us but not for God."[6] I don't know of any traditional theist who puts it this way. Some have spoken of "apparent contradictions," but that is quite different from "genuine contradictions for us." The latter phrase certainly makes no sense. Contradictions are either apparent or genuine, not genuine for somebody and not genuine for somebody else. When traditional theologians speak of apparent contradictions, they mean to deny that these are real or genuine to anybody. They merely wish to disclaim the ability to show the consistency of the doctrines under discussion. Would that theologians were more often willing to confess their inabilities! Surely no objection can be lodged against such extraordinary and becoming modesty.

In this and other ways, Sanders's discussion of logic is confused. But the abstract concept of apparent contradiction is less important than the open theists' substantive claims that contradictions exist in traditional theology. Sanders considers contradictory, for example, the traditional view that "the

3. John Sanders, *The God Who Risks* (Downers Grove, Ill.: InterVarsity Press, 1998), 36.
4. I shall discuss these definitions of freedom in chapter 8.
5. Sanders, *The God Who Risks*, 34–36.
6. Ibid., 36.

Bible teaches both exhaustive divine control over all events and that humans remain morally responsible."[7] Pinnock characteristically makes the point with rhetorical flourish:

> To say that God hates sin while secretly willing it, to say that God warns us not to fall away though it is impossible, to say that God loves the world while excluding most people from the opportunity of salvation, to say that God warmly invites sinners to come knowing all the while that they cannot possibly do so—such things do not deserve to be called mysteries when that is just a euphemism for nonsense.[8]

I will argue in chapter 7 that these criticisms fail to make a proper distinction between God's preceptive and decretive wills, and in chapter 8 that God sometimes has good reasons for bringing about things that he hates. If these arguments are sound, they adequately answer the charge of logical contradiction.

 We cannot judge whether two statements are contradictory until we have an adequate understanding of what they mean. Statements sometimes look contradictory until we analyze them carefully. When one person says it is raining, and another person says it is not, their reports appear contradictory. But if we discover a heavy mist outside, we may judge that both statements describe the weather equally well. All logic textbooks recognize that fact. The law of noncontradiction says that A is never not-A *at the same time and in the same respect.* The "same respect" qualification implies that we must understand the meanings of terms before we can judge expressions to be contradictory. We must not judge statements to be contradictory

7. Ibid.

8. Clark H. Pinnock, "Systematic Theology," in OG, 115. He cites David Basinger, "Biblical Paradox: Does Revelation Change Logic?" *Journal of the Evangelical Theological Society* 30 (1987): 205–13.

simply because they look contradictory at first glance. So the issue is not really logic, but theological substance.

Models

Sanders expounds a "risk model of providence," rather than the "'no-risk' view" of traditional theology.[9] He admits that *risk taker* is a metaphor, rather than a literal description of God, but he thinks it is an important metaphor to emphasize in the present context. More traditional metaphors, such as *king,* he thinks, obscure various aspects of God's relationship to us.[10]

Models, then, are metaphors that help us to organize in a unified conception many of the particular things we know about God. A single model is never exhaustive. We learn about God from the full teaching of Scripture, not by extrapolating ideas from a model. Our exegesis of Scripture must control our models, not the reverse. Given our finitude, however, we cannot think of everything in the Bible at once. So organizing biblical data into various general concepts and models is a necessary aspect of theological work.

I shall explore Sanders's "risk taker" model later in this book, concluding that it is unscriptural. Even at this preliminary stage in our discussion, however, the reader should have some doubts about this model. Scripture never actually speaks of God as a risk taker, but speaks of him as King and Lord thousands of times. The notion that God is a risk taker is, at best, a deduction from certain debatable interpretations, whereas the idea that he is King and Lord is clearly a central emphasis of the biblical writers' own doctrine of God.[11]

Risk taker vs King/Lord.
Is the Lord of Heaven & Earth

9. Sanders, *The God Who Risks,* 10.
10. Ibid., 11.
11. See my justification for treating the doctrine of God as the theology of lordship in my forthcoming *The Doctrine of God,* chaps. 1–6. The title Lord represents God's very name, Yahweh.

Sanders does relate the idea of God as a risk taker to the concept of divine repentance or relenting, which, to be sure, can be found a few times in Scripture. I shall argue later that divine relenting, understood biblically, does not imply risk taking. But there is still a huge disproportion between the biblical uses of *relent* in connection with God and the uses of *King* and *Lord.*

The idea that *risk taker* could actually replace *king* as a controlling metaphor strikes me as absurd. It is utterly wrongheaded and extremely dangerous. As we shall see, this procedure introduces massive distortions into theology. But it is essential to open theism. Indeed, it is simply another way of expressing the main principle of open theism, which is that everything must conform to the doctrine of libertarian freedom. If man is to be free in this sense, then God cannot control the future. If God is to act at all, he must take risks. And in a world of libertarian freedom, God's kingship, his lordship, becomes problematic. It becomes a metaphor best avoided, so that the model of risk taker may be clearly understood.

 The selection of a controlling model, therefore, is a kind of presupposition. It determines the course of a theological discussion at the outset. Although I have many exegetical differences with the open theists, my most serious objections concern the presuppositions that they bring to the text, the presuppositions that govern their exegesis.

Straightforward Exegesis and Anthropomorphism

One of the debates between open theists and traditional theologians has to do with whether the references in Scripture to God's "repentance," "changing his mind," "growing in knowledge," etc., should be taken literally or figuratively. Ware says:

> One of the initial appeals of the openness proposal is its challenge that we take the text of Scripture simply for what

it says. Stop making it say the opposite of what it so clearly and plainly does say, openness proponents argue. When the Lord says to Abraham . . . "for now I know that you fear God" (Gen. 22:12), we should allow these words to speak and mean exactly what normal conversational speech would convey. That is, God truly and literally learned what he previously had not known.[12]

Openness writers often speak of this principle as "straightforward" exegesis. Traditional theologians, however, have often described such passages as "anthropomorphic": describing God as if he were a man. On the traditional view, God has perfect knowledge of the future, and therefore he could not literally learn anything new.

Ware points out that the so-called straightforward interpretation of Genesis 22:12 cannot be maintained, even in the system of open theism. He makes three points. First, if God literally needed to test Abraham to find out what was in Abraham's heart, then his ignorance was not of the future, but of the present. But open theists often claim that God knows the present exhaustively. Second, this interpretation denies what open theists elsewhere affirm, that God knows the inner motivations of the human heart. Third, if God is trying to find out whether Abraham will be faithful in the future, he is trying to know Abraham's libertarian free choices in advance, which, on the openness view, not even God can know.

I agree with Ware that we should generally follow the surface meaning of a text unless there is reason to do otherwise.[13] But exegetical controversies are often about such reasons. We cannot resolve such controversies without evaluating these reasons. It will not help simply to claim that a certain interpretation is the straightforward one. In Ware's example,

12. Bruce A. Ware, *God's Lesser Glory* (Wheaton, Ill.: Crossway Books, 2000), 65.
13. Ibid., 66.

both open theists and traditional theists have reason not to interpret the text literally, although the open theists have not always been aware of the reasons on their side.

Exegesis of these texts must take into account both their surface meaning and what the rest of Scripture teaches about God. Traditional theology acknowledges this point, for it regards such texts as Genesis 22:12 as anthropomorphic on the basis of its overall view of God's knowledge. Open theists should likewise be concerned to understand the text in the light of their other assertions, though often they are not. At least they should be more concerned about the logical consistency between their interpretation of Genesis 22:12 and their other assertions about God. In any case, it is simplistic merely to say that traditional theology treats these texts anthropomorphically, while open theism treats them straightforwardly.

Indeed, it is simplistic to divide all interpretations into the categories of "anthropomorphic" and "literal." All biblical references to God are anthropomorphic in the sense that they speak of God in human language, use concepts that are at least somewhat understandable to human beings, and make some comparison, at least implicitly, between God and human beings. And all such references are literal in that, rightly understood, they present God as he really and truly is.

In many ways, indeed, God is literally like a man. For example, men speak, and God also speaks, although in many ways his speaking is different from man's. And, as we shall see, when God enters history (as in the Incarnation, but not only then), he experiences the flow of time as we do: he sees one thing happening on Monday and another on Tuesday. Scriptural references to God's acts in time are anthropomorphic, but not merely anthropomorphic.[14]

14. For more discussion of literal, figurative, metaphorical, analogical, and anthropomorphic predication, see my *The Doctrine of the Knowledge of God*, 18–40, 226–32; *Cornelius Van Til*, 161–75; *The Doctrine of God*, chap. 11.

FOUR

Is Love God's Most Important Attribute?

In the remainder of this book, I shall examine the main contentions of open theism that I summarized in chapter 1, though not always in the precise order of that list. First, I will consider the first contention on the list, namely, that love is God's most important quality.

God's qualities, often called attributes, are ideas expressed by nouns (as *eternity*) or adjectives (as *eternal*) by which we describe God. Some of these attributes, in traditional theology, are infinity, eternity, immensity, unchangeability, omnipotence, omniscience, omnipresence, wisdom, goodness, justice, holiness, truth, and love.

Some theologians have tried to show that one attribute of God (or a group of attributes) uniquely describes his essence and therefore is more fundamental than the others. In some cases, they have tried to deduce some or all of the other attributes from the fundamental attribute. For Aquinas, the proper name of God is Being. So Aquinas deduces many, perhaps all, of God's attributes from the premise that God's essence is identical to his being *(esse,* "existence"). Herman

Bavinck surveys other such attempts in the history of theology: for Duns Scotus, God's fundamental attribute is his infinity; for some Reformed theologians, aseity;[1] for Cornelius Jansenius, veracity; for Saint-Cyran, omnipotence; for the Socinians, will; for Hegel, reason; for Jacobi, Lotze, Dorner, and others, absolute personality; for Ritschl, love.[2] Among theologians since Bavinck's day, we can note Barth's emphasis on "love in freedom,"[3] Buber's and Brunner's "person,"[4] and Moltmann's "futurity."[5]

On this question, open theists take the position of Ritschl, regarding love as God's fundamental attribute.[6] Certainly that is tempting, because of the statement that "God is love" in 1 John 4:8 and 16, and because of the centrality in biblical ethics of that love that imitates God's love (Ex. 20:1–3; Deut. 6:4–9; John 13:34–35; 1 Cor. 13; Phil. 2:1–11; 1 John 3:16; 4:10). But does "God is love" describe anything more fundamental in God than "God is light" (1 John 1:5) or "God is spirit" (John 4:24)? Or does it describe God's nature more perfectly than the exposition of God's name (in terms of both love and wrath) in Exodus 34:6–7? What about "the LORD, whose name is Jealous" in Exodus 34:14 (cf. 20:5)? Or "the Holy One of Israel" (Pss. 71:22; 78:41; 89:18; Isa. 1:4 and of-

---

1. Gordon H. Clark proposes a logical deduction of all God's attributes from the attribute of aseity. See his "Attributes, the Divine," in *Baker's Dictionary of Theology,* ed. Everett F. Harrison (Grand Rapids: Baker, 1960), 78–79.

2. Herman Bavinck, *The Doctrine of God* (Grand Rapids: Baker, 1951), 114–20.

3. Karl Barth, *Church Dogmatics* (Edinburgh: T. and T. Clark, 1936–60), II/1–2.

4. Martin Buber, *I and Thou* (Edinburgh: T. and T. Clark, 1937); Emil Brunner, *Dogmatics I, The Christian Doctrine of God* (London: Lutterworth Press, 1949).

5. Jürgen Moltmann, *The Theology of Hope* (New York: Harper and Row, 1965).

6. Ritschl lived from 1822 to 1889. So this element of open theism, like those discussed in chapter 2, is not uniquely contemporary.

---

ten in Isaiah; note its threefold repetition in Isa. 6:3)? Or almightiness, the attribute given to God in the patriarchal name El Shaddai? What about Exodus 33:19, where God expounds his name in terms of the sovereignty of his mercy ("I will have mercy on whom I will have mercy, and I will have compassion on whom I will have compassion")? It is easier to argue the centrality of an attribute when one does not try to make specific comparisons with other attributes. But *centrality* and *importance* are comparative terms. To argue the relative importance of a divine attribute requires precisely such comparisons.

In my forthcoming book *The Doctrine of God,* the title Lord plays a central role. Certainly Lord is the most fundamental name of God in Scripture, and all biblical revelation expounds it. God performs his mighty acts so that people "will know that I am the LORD" (Ex. 6:7; cf. 7:5, 17; 8:22, and many other verses throughout Scripture). So his lordship is the attribute most often mentioned in Scripture, by the constant use of the Hebrew *yahweh* and *adon* and the Greek *kyrios.* For pedagogical purposes, and for purposes of edification, it makes good sense to start where Scripture starts and emphasize what Scripture emphasizes, especially since God's lordship leads so easily to a consideration of other topics. Yet I would not want to say that lordship is metaphysically central to God's nature in a way that holiness, love, eternity, and righteousness are not. These other concepts can also be central in specific biblical contexts. They also can name God, and even define him, as in 1 John 1:5 and 4:8.

Rather than making any single attribute central, classical theology teaches that all of God's defining attributes[7] are ways of describing his simple essence. So God's attributes are not

7. By "defining attributes" I am referring to attributes that define God's nature. There are some attributes outside this category, like "creator of John Smith."

parts or divisions within his nature, but each attribute is necessary to his being. Each is essential to him, and therefore his essence includes all of them. God cannot be God without his goodness, his wisdom, his eternity, or his love. In other words, he is necessarily good, wise, eternal, and loving. None of his attributes can be removed from him, and no new attribute can be added to him. Not one attribute exists without the others. So each attribute has divine attributes; each is qualified by the others. God's wisdom is an eternal wisdom; his goodness is a wise goodness and a just goodness.

So in *The Doctrine of God* I argue that the essential attributes of God are "perspectival." That is, each of them describes everything that God is, from a different perspective. In one sense, any attribute may be taken as central, and the others seen in relation to it. But in that sense, the doctrine of God has many centers, not just one. Theologians are wrong when they think that the centrality of their favorite attribute excludes the centrality of others. These writers are (as often among theologians) right in what they assert, but wrong in what they deny. Ritschl is right to say that love is God's essence, but wrong to deny that holiness is. And that kind of error is sometimes linked to other theological errors. Often when a theologian makes God's love central, in contrast to other attributes, he intends, contrary to Scripture, to cast doubt on the reality or intensity of God's wrath and judgment. That was the case with Ritschl, and it is the case with some modern evangelicals.[8]

I am not saying that all attributes are equally important to our understanding of God. One writer says that God is a "knitter" in Psalm 139:15.[9] Well, I suppose that on that basis we should recognize "knitting capacity" as a divine attri-

8. See the excellent critique of their position by Robert A. Peterson, *Hell on Trial* (Phillipsburg, N.J.: P&R Publishing, 1995). As we shall see, many of the open theists question the traditional doctrine of eternal punishment.
9. Leland Ryken, James C. Wilhoit, and Tremper Longman III, *Dictionary of Biblical Imagery* (Downers Grove, Ill.: InterVarsity Press, 1998), 334.

bute. But of course that attribute would not be as important as love or omnipotence. It would be a perspective on all of God's attributes, for all of God's work is the knitting of a tapestry to set forth his glory. But it is not the most important perspective in Scripture.

So we should ask if the primacy of love can be taken in a somewhat weaker sense: not that love is metaphysically primary, but that it is primary in our understanding of God. This time, we are not asking whether love alone is God's essence, but whether Scripture emphasizes love more prominently than his other qualities. But to argue even for this conclusion is very difficult in view of the other biblical candidates for chief attribute that we saw earlier: light, Spirit, jealousy, holiness, almightiness, sovereign compassion, lordship. To establish the open theist conclusion, one would have to show, not only that love is important, not only that it is perspectivally central as in the above discussion, but that it is somehow more important to the biblical revelation than each of the other candidates. To my knowledge, no open theist has even begun that difficult task.

Richard Rice summarizes much biblical evidence for the importance of divine love (e.g., 1 John 4:8–10, 15–16; Ps. 103:8; Isa. 54:8; Deut. 7:8; Jer. 31:3; Isa. 63:9; Rom. 8:32; 5:8; John 3:16), and he quotes Heschel, Barth, Brunner, Kasper, and Pannenberg in support. Certainly these texts show that God's love is important. But Rice wants to argue more, that it is "more important than all of God's other attributes," even "more fundamental." He says, "Love is the essence of the divine reality, the basic source from which *all* of God's attributes arise."[10] But never does he actually present any comparisons between love and any other divine attributes. Just to show the importance and centrality of love in Scripture does not justify that conclusion. One must also

10. Richard Rice, "Biblical Support for a New Perspective," in OG, 21.

show that other attributes are less important and less central than love. But Rice's discussion never touches on any divine attribute other than love.

It is especially difficult to make a scriptural case that God's love is more important than his lordship. The NIV uses the word *lord* 7,484 times, to give only a rough measure of the term's importance. "LORD" is the translation of the covenant name that God gave to Moses in Exodus 3:13–15. God regularly performs mighty deeds so that people "will know that I am the LORD" (Ex. 6:7; 7:5, 17; 8:22; 10:2; 14:4, 18, and often throughout the Old Testament). The fundamental Christian confession is "Jesus Christ is Lord" (Rom. 10:9; 1 Cor. 12:3; Phil. 2:11; cf. John 20:28; Acts 2:36). Of course, God's lordship in Scripture is not opposed to his love. It includes it, and includes all of God's other attributes as well.

Even if open theists could show that love is God's most important attribute, they would then raise the further question of what love is. For we have seen that every defining attribute of God includes all the others. God's love is a righteous love, an eternal love, a sovereign love. I gather that open theists maintain the primacy of love in part because they want to deny the primacy of attributes like omnipotence and unchangeability, not to mention justice and wrath. But if love includes these other attributes, if God's love is omnipotent and unchangeable, then open theists accomplish very little by making love primary.

Nobody will deny that God's love is very important in Scripture and provides a legitimate perspective for learning other things about him. But open theists should be reminded that whatever they may think about the relative importance of love, they are nevertheless responsible to do full justice to everything else that the Bible says about God. To do that, it is important to look at him from many perspectives.

Love, Sensitivity, Responsiveness, and Vulnerability

In describing the nature of divine love, the main concern of the open theists is to emphasize that "love is more than care and commitment; it involves being sensitive and responsive as well."[11] Evidently, they do not believe that traditional theology affirms, or emphasizes sufficiently, these qualities of love.

Classical theology does not usually employ these terms, but it certainly does affirm the ideas expressed by them. To be sensitive is to be moved by the "attitudes, feelings, or circumstances of others."[12] To be responsive is to act in a gracious way, appropriate to those attitudes, feelings, and circumstances. Certainly the God of classical theology knows exhaustively the attitudes, feelings, and circumstances of his creatures. And that God acts graciously in accordance with that knowledge. Indeed, as we shall see more fully later, God himself feels. Charles Hodge wrote, "Love of necessity involves feeling, and if there be no feeling in God, there can be no love."[13]

I shall discuss later how a supratemporal God can respond to temporal events and circumstances. (As I indicated earlier, I do not dismiss this responsiveness as "merely anthropomorphic.") But surely there is nothing in classical theology to prevent God from having a sympathetic understanding of our condition, and there is nothing to prevent him from acting in love to deliver us from our woes. His power, knowledge, and omnipresence make him the truest and nearest friend to all who call on him in faith. What more can anyone legitimately ask for in the name of love?

Perhaps what the open theists really want from God is "vulnerability," which Pinnock associates with the love of God in

11. Ibid., 15.
12. *The American Heritage College Dictionary* (Boston: Houghton Mifflin, 2000), 1242.
13. Charles Hodge, *Systematic Theology* (reprint, Grand Rapids: Eerdmans, n.d.), 1:428–29.

a passage I quoted in chapter 1.[14] I shall argue in chapter 11 that there is a sense even in classical theology in which God is vulnerable: he exposed himself to death in the incarnation of Christ. But classical theology also affirms that God is invulnerable in the sense that he cannot suffer loss to his nature or defeat in accomplishing his eternal plan. Open theism is evidently not satisfied with that traditional understanding. It demands a further level of vulnerability as an aspect of divine love.

But what about that? Must someone be vulnerable in order to love you? Or for you to love him? Someone's vulnerability may lead you to sympathize with him or to pity him, and those emotions can get mixed up with love in various ways. But is it really impossible to recognize love in someone who is too strong to be defeated? On the contrary, do we not desire in a lover precisely the kind of strength that will not fail to support us—the kind of love that will hold us fast, from which nothing can separate us? Certainly that is the nature of God's love in Scripture. Nothing can separate us from the love of Christ (Rom. 8:35). Nobody can pluck us out of his hand (John 10:28–29). God's love is a *sovereign* love—not, in the final analysis, a vulnerable love.

14. Clark H. Pinnock, "Systematic Theology," in OG, 103.

Is God's Will the Ultimate Explanation of Everything?

As we have seen, open theists deny that God's will is the ultimate explanation of everything. Their view is that "history is the combined result of what God and his creatures decide to do."[1] I shall discuss later the role of creatures in the historical process: the nature of their freedom (chapter 8) and whether they can be said to influence God (chapters 10 and 11). In this chapter, however, I intend to present the biblical basis for the view that God's will is indeed the ultimate explanation of everything.[2] In this chapter, I will not refer much to the open theists, but in the next chapter I will consider their objections to the doctrine of God's universal foreordination.

---

1. Richard Rice, "Biblical Support for a New Perspective," in OG, 16.
2. A couple of technical points: (1) The expression "God's will" here should not be taken to suggest that God's will is more fundamental than his intellect or some other divine faculty. I use the phrase here by way of accommodation to the language of the open theists; I could just as easily say that God himself is the ultimate explanation. (2) "God's will" in this chapter refers to God's decretive will, not his preceptive will. For this distinction, see chapter 7.

The Natural World

The biblical writers do not hesitate to ascribe the events of the natural world directly to God. *He* waters the land (Ps. 65:9–11). *He* sends the lightning and the wind (Ps. 135:5–7). *He* spreads the snow, frost, and hail, and then sends out his word to melt them (Ps. 147:15–18). Compare Gen. 8:22; Job 38–40; Pss. 104:10–30; 107:23–32; 145:15–16; 147:8–9; Acts 14:17, and many other passages. God does not merely allow these things to happen; he makes them happen.

Even those events that appear to be most random are under God's sovereign control: "The lot is cast into the lap, but its every decision is from the LORD" (Prov. 16:33). What we call "accidents" come from the Lord (Ex. 21:13; Judg. 9:53; 1 Kings 22:34).

Sometimes God brings about natural events with purposeful discrimination. When he sent hail upon the Egyptians as a punishment for Pharaoh's disobedience, he left untouched the land of Goshen, where the Israelites lived (Ex. 9:13–26). He gives rain to one town and withholds it from another (Amos 4:7). He is the one who sends both prosperity and famine (Gen. 41:32).

Jesus emphasizes that God's control of nature extends to the smallest details. He says that our Father not only makes the sun rise and sends rain (Matt. 5:45), but also feeds the birds (6:26–27), clothes the lilies (6:28–30), accounts for the falling sparrows (10:29), and numbers the hairs on our head (10:30).

So the biblical view of the natural world is intensely personalistic. Natural events come from God. This is not to deny that there are forces in nature itself, perhaps even "natural laws" in some sense, though it would be hard to prove the existence of such laws from Scripture. But behind all the forces of nature itself is the force of the personal Lord.

Human History

God made us from dust (Gen. 2:7), and so we are a part of nature and dependent on the rain, the sunshine, the crops, and the animals. Without the cooperation of the "lower creation," we could not exist. When Jesus talks about God providing for the sparrows and lilies, it is part of an *a fortiori* argument: *how much more* does he care for you? We are "worth more than many sparrows" (Matt. 10:31).

Nor could we exist without a vast accumulation of apparently random events. We all owe our existence to the combination of one sperm and one egg, out of a vast number of possible combinations, and to equally improbable combinations that produced each of our parents and our ancestors back to Adam. And consider how many natural events enabled each of our ancestors to survive to maturity and reproduce. All of these things, plus the improbable events of our own life experience, have made us what we are.

So if God controls all the events of nature, then certainly he also controls the course of our own life. And we do not need to infer that conclusion from the preceding discussion; rather, Scripture teaches it explicitly. The apostle Paul tells the Athenian philosophers, "From one man [God] made every nation of men, that they should inhabit the whole earth; and he determined the times set for them and the exact places where they should live" (Acts 17:26). God is King, not only over Israel, but over all the nations, over all the earth (Pss. 45:6–12; 47:1–9; 95:3; cf. Gen. 18:25). He governs the events of human history for his purposes (Ps. 33:10–11).

Consider some of the ways in which God governs the great events of history. We are familiar with the story of Joseph, who is betrayed by his brothers and sold into slavery in Egypt, but later is elevated to a position of prominence. God uses him as the means to preserve his family in Egypt, where they become a great nation. The Genesis narrative ascribes all these events to the Lord.

Joseph interprets Pharaoh's two dreams as indicating seven prosperous years, followed by seven years of famine. Joseph denies that he has any innate ability to interpret dreams: "I cannot do it, but God will give Pharaoh the answer he desires" (Gen. 41:16). God is not only the interpreter of the dream, but also its subject. Joseph says, "God has shown Pharaoh what he is about to do . . . and God will do it soon" (vv. 28, 32). It is God who will bring prosperity and then famine.

Even the betrayal of Joseph by his brothers is the Lord's work. It is God who sends Joseph to Egypt to save lives, and it is God who makes Joseph a ruler in Egypt (Gen. 45:5–8). Joseph realizes that his brothers intended to harm him, but "God intended it for good to accomplish what is now being done, the saving of many lives" (50:20).[3]

It is God who brings his people out of Egypt by his strong arm. Then he puts terror into the hearts of Israel's enemies as his people take their inheritance in the Promised Land (Ex. 23:27; Deut. 2:25; cf. Gen. 35:5). After Joshua's conquests, God gives them rest, keeping all his promises (Josh. 21:44–45). In warfare, it is always the Lord who gives victory (Deut. 3:22; Josh. 24:11; 1 Sam. 17:47; 2 Chron. 20:15; Prov. 21:31; Zech. 4:6).

When Israel forsakes the Lord, he uses the Assyrians and the Babylonians as his tools to accomplish his sure purposes (Isa. 14:26–27; cf. 10:5–12; 14:24–25; 37:26), but he will humble those nations, too, in his own time (Jer. 29:11–14).

---

3. John Sanders, in *The God Who Risks* (Downers Grove, Ill.: InterVarsity Press, 1998), 55, insists that "the text does not say that God caused or necessitated these events," despite the word "intended." Rather, in Sanders's view, the text says only that God brought good out of evil. But Sanders offers no argument for his interpretation, which contradicts not only the straightforward meaning of the text, but the sustained contextual emphasis on divine agency.

No Other God

It is the Lord who "sets up kings and deposes them" (Dan. 2:21; cf. 4:34–35). He names the Persian emperor Cyrus, centuries before his birth, and appoints him to bring Israel back to the Promised Land (Isa. 44:28; 45:1–13). Then God moves his heart (Ezra 1:1) to order the return. Years before Cyrus's edict, God said "I will" do this (Jer. 30:4–24).

All of these events set the stage for the coming of Jesus (Gal. 4:4). Again, God brings everything about. Jesus' conception is supernatural. Everything he does fulfills prophecy (e.g., Matt. 1:22; 2:15; 3:3; 4:14). He is betrayed, but that betrayal itself is the result of "God's set purpose and foreknowledge" (Acts 2:23–24; cf. 3:18; 4:27–28; 13:27; Luke 22:22). And it is God the Father who raises Jesus from the dead, and who has planned the day and hour of his return (Matt. 24:36).

Thus, God rules the whole course of human history. Scripture, of course, focuses on the great events of the history of redemption: God's election of Israel, and the incarnation, death, resurrection, ascension, and return of Jesus. But for these great events to take place, God has to be in control of all the nations—Egypt, Babylon, Assyria, and Persia, as well as Israel. And he has to be in control of all the forces of nature, apart from which the events of history cannot take place. Indeed, his mighty deeds prove him to be no less than King over all the earth.

Individual Human Lives

But God does not control only the course of nature and the great events of history. As we have seen, he is also concerned with details. So we find in Scripture that God controls the course of each person's life. How could it be otherwise? God controls all natural events in detail, even including apparently random events. He controls the history of nations and of human salvation. But these, in turn, govern to a large extent the events of our daily lives. Conversely, if God does not control a vast number of individual human lives, it is hard to imagine how he would be able to control the great developments of history.

In fact, Scripture teaches explicitly that God controls the course of our individual lives. That control begins before we are conceived in the womb, as with Jeremiah (Jer. 1:5). If God knew Jeremiah before his conception, then God must have arranged for one particular sperm to reach one particular egg to produce each of Jeremiah's ancestors back to Adam, and then Jeremiah himself. So God is in control of all the "accidents" of history to create the precise person he seeks to employ as his prophet.[4] God's foreknowledge of one individual implies comprehensive control over the entire human family. Paul says of all believers that God "chose us in [Christ] before the creation of the world" (Eph. 1:4).

So the whole history of human procreation is under God's control, as he acts intentionally to bring about the conception of each one of us (Gen. 4:1, 25; 18:13–14; 25:21; 29:31–30:2; 30:17, 23–24; Deut. 10:22; Ruth 4:13; Pss. 113:9; 127:3–5). And of course God is also active after each child's conception, as he is formed in the womb (Ps. 139:4–6).

So we owe our very existence as human beings to God's gift of life. Furthermore, we are who we are as individuals by God's providence. Modern science continues to discover more and more things about us that arise because of our genetic makeup, through the incredibly complex programming of the DNA code.[5] How could anything but a personal cre-

4. The same must be said of Cyrus, discussed earlier. Also, according to 1 Kings 13:1–3, an unnamed prophet told wicked King Jeroboam that a son of David named Josiah would kill his idolatrous priests. As in the case of Cyrus, the prophet mentioned Josiah by name, along with his activities, long before his birth (1 Kings 13:1–3).

5. I do not believe, however, that the genetic code accounts for everything we are. There are complex relationships between body and spirit.

No Other God

ator account for such information technology within every living cell?

After birth, too, the events of our lives are in God's hands. Exodus 21:12–13, a law concerning the taking of life, reads:

> Anyone who strikes a man and kills him shall surely be put to death. However, if he does not do it intentionally, but God lets it happen, he is to flee to a place I will designate.

Here the law ascribes what we would call "accidental" loss of life to the agency of God. Naomi, the mother-in-law of Ruth, sees the hand of God in the death of her two sons (Ruth 1:13). In the prayer of Hannah, the mother of Samuel, she recognizes the hand of God:

> The LORD brings death and makes alive;
>   he brings down to the grave and raises up.
> The LORD sends poverty and wealth;
>   he humbles and he exalts. (1 Sam. 2:6–7;
>   cf. Ps. 37:23)

So God plans the course of our lives: our birth, our death, and whether we prosper or not.[6]

The differences among us—our different natural and spiritual abilities—come from God (Rom. 12:3–6; 1 Cor. 4:7; 12:4–6).

James tells us not to be too sure about our future, for that is entirely in the Lord's hands (James 4:13–16).[7] Clearly, all the events of our lives are in God's hands. Whatever we do depends on God's willing it to happen.

---

6. I shall have more to say about God's foreordination of the specific evils in our lives in a discussion of the problem of evil in chapter 8.

7. For a negative example, see Jesus' parable of the rich fool in Luke 12:13–21. Compare also Jer. 10:23, "I know, O LORD, that a man's life is not his own; it is not for man to direct his steps."

Human Decisions

We now approach a more controversial area, that of human decisions. Does God bring about our decisions? Some of them? Any of them? In chapter 8, I shall discuss the nature of human responsibility and freedom, which are genuine and important. But here we must face the fact that our decisions are not independent of God, and therefore that our definition of freedom must somehow be consistent with God's sovereignty over the human will.

In our survey of the history of redemption, we saw that God brought about the free decisions of certain people, such as Joseph's brothers (Gen. 45:5–8), Cyrus (Isa. 44:28), and Judas (Luke 22:22; Acts 2:23–24; 3:18; 4:27–28; 13:27). So we should not be prejudiced by the unbiblical, but popular notion that God never foreordains our free decisions.

Furthermore, we have seen that God ordains the events of nature and the events of our daily life. How can such pervasive divine involvement in our life not profoundly influence our decisions? It is God who has made us, inside and out. To make us who we are, he must control our heredity. So he has given us the parents we have, and their parents, and their parents. And to give us our parents, God had to control many of their free decisions (such as the free decision of Jeremiah's parents to marry) and those of their parents, grandparents, etc. Moreover, we have seen that God has placed us in our environment, in the situations that require us to make decisions. He decides how long we shall live and brings about our successes and failures, even though such events usually depend on our free decisions, in addition to outside factors.

Negatively, God's purposes exclude many free decisions that would otherwise be possible. Since God had planned to bring Joseph to Egypt, his brothers were, in an important sense, not free to kill him, although at one point they planned to do so. Nor could Goliath have killed David, nor could Jeremiah have died in the womb. Nor could the Roman soldiers have broken Jesus' legs when he hung on the cross, for God's prophets had declared otherwise.

But, over and above these inferences,[8] Scripture teaches directly that God brings about our free decisions. He does not foreordain merely what happens to us, but also what we choose to do.

The root of human decision is the *heart.* Jesus says that both good and evil things come from the heart (Luke 6:45). But that heart is under God's control: "The king's heart is in the hand of the LORD; he directs it like a watercourse wherever he pleases" (Prov. 21:1). Certainly this is what God did with Cyrus, as we have seen. It is also what he did with the pharaoh of the Exodus (Rom. 9:17; cf. Ex. 9:16; 14:4), as we shall see in the next section.[9]

God directs the heart, not only of kings, but of all people (Ps. 33:15). So he controls the decisions, not only of Pharaoh, but also of the Egyptian people, giving them a favorable disposition toward Israel (Ex. 12:36). Scripture underscores that this change was the Lord's work, for it mentions that God had predicted it in his meeting with Moses at the burning bush (Ex. 3:21–22).

God, who forms the purposes of our heart, also decides the steps we will take to carry out those purposes:

> In his heart a man plans his course,
>   but the LORD determines his steps. (Prov. 16:9;
>   cf. 16:1; 19:21)

---

8. Another inference may be made on the basis of God's exhaustive knowledge of the future. If God knows our free decisions before we are born, then certainly we are not the ultimate source of them. However, open theists deny God's exhaustive knowledge of the future, so I shall have to defend that doctrine at a later point (chap. 12). If that defense is cogent, it provides another argument for the thesis of this chapter.

9. See also 1 Sam. 10:9 on Saul and 1 Kings 3:12 on Solomon.

According to many Scripture passages, God controls our free decisions and attitudes, often predicting those decisions far in advance. He declared that when the Israelites went up to Jerusalem for the annual feasts, the enemy nations would not covet their land (Ex. 34:24). God was saying that he would control the minds and hearts of these pagan peoples so that they would not cause trouble for Israel at those times.

When Gideon led his tiny army against the Midianite camp, "the LORD caused the men throughout the camp to turn on each other with their swords" (Judg. 7:22). During the Exile, God "caused" a chief Babylonian official "to show favor and sympathy to Daniel" (Dan. 1:9). After the Exile, the Lord "filled [Israel] with joy by changing the attitude of the king of Assyria " (Ezra 6:22).

The soldiers at Jesus' crucifixion freely decided not to tear Jesus' garment, but instead to cast lots for it. But God had foreordained this decision:

> This happened that the scripture might be fulfilled which said,
>
> "They divided my garments among them
>   and cast lots for my clothing." (John 19:24, quoting Ps. 22:18; cf. John 19:31–37)

John's point is not only that God knew in advance what would happen, but rather that the event took place *so that* the Scriptures might be fulfilled. Whose intention was it to fulfill Scripture through this event? It was not the intent of the soldiers, but the intent of God, the primary cause of their decision.

The Gospels tell us over and over again that things happen so that Scripture may be fulfilled. Many of those events involve free decisions of human beings (see, e.g., Matt. 1:20–23; 2:14–15, 22–23; 4:12–16). In some cases, human beings (such as Jesus himself in 4:12–16) may have consciously intended to fulfill Scripture. In other cases, they either had no such intention or did not even know they were fulfilling Scripture (e.g., Matt. 21:1–5; 26:55–56; Acts 13:27–29). In any case, Scripture must be fulfilled (Mark 14:49).[10]

The picture given to us by this large group of passages is that God's purpose stands behind the free decisions of human beings. Often God tells us, sometimes long before the event, what a human being will freely decide to do. But the point is not merely that God has advance knowledge of an event, but that he is fulfilling his own purpose through that event. That divine purpose imparts a certain necessity (Gk. *dei*, as in, e.g., Matt. 16:21; 24:6; Mark 8:31; 9:11; 13:7, 10, 14; Luke 9:22; 17:25; 24:26) to the human decision to bring about the predicted event.[11] We shall, of course, have to discuss later how this necessity is compatible with human freedom.

Sins

This section raises even more serious difficulties than the last. If it is hard for us to accept God's foreordination of human decisions and actions in general, it is even harder to accept his foreordination of our sinful decisions and actions in

---

10. In this passage, Jesus says that Scripture was fulfilled both in the decision of his enemies not to try to arrest him in the temple courts and in their decision to arrest him in the garden. Both, of course, were free decisions.

11. The nature of "fulfillment" in reference to prophecy is rather complex. Sometimes, as in Deut. 18:21–22 and Dan. 7:1–28, prophecy straightforwardly predicts future events and is fulfilled when those events take place. In other cases, as in Matt. 2:14–15, the relationship between prophecy and fulfillment is not as evident. When Matthew quotes Hos. 11:1, "Out of Egypt I called my son," he is not claiming, I think, that Hosea predicted the Messiah's sojourn in Egypt, but rather that that sojourn is symbolically appropriate to Jesus' role as the faithful remnant of Israel. But in any case, the text suggests that God was bringing about an event that in one way or another (literally, allusively, or symbolically) brought out the depth of meaning in the prophecy. In these fulfillment passages, there is always a sense of divine necessity.

---

particular. The former raises questions about human freedom and responsibility; the latter raises questions about God's own goodness. For how can a holy God bring about sin?

That is the notorious "problem of evil." There is no perfectly satisfying solution to it. Some have tried to solve it by appealing to libertarian freedom, but I shall try to show later that such an appeal is inadequate, since freedom in the libertarian sense is both unscriptural and destructive to moral responsibility. It is more helpful to point out that Scripture itself regards this problem as a mystery (Job 38–42), and that God has a supremely good purpose for ordaining evil that one day will silence all his critics and evoke praise (Rom. 8:28–39; 9:17–24; Rev. 15:3–4).[12]

But for now, it is important to see that God does in fact bring about the sinful behavior of human beings, whatever problems that may create in our understanding. However we address the problem of evil, our response must be in accord with the great number of Scripture passages that affirm God's foreordination of everything, even including sin. Many attempts to solve the problem of evil deny this premise, but it is clearly taught in Scripture.

We have already seen that God controls the free decisions of human beings, particularly by controlling the heart, the center of human existence. But the hearts of fallen people are sinful, as God says through Jeremiah (Jer. 17:9). People freely choose to do evil, since they act in accord with their true desire—but for that they are no less under God's control.

So we saw that God sent Joseph into Egypt to preserve his family in a time of famine, accomplishing that by means of

12. For a longer discussion of the problem of evil, see my *Apologetics to the Glory of God* (Phillipsburg, N.J.: P&R Publishing, 1994), 149–90, and my forthcoming *The Doctrine of God*, chap. 9. I shall discuss the problem in chapter 8 of this book in connection with the role of human freedom.

the sinful actions of Joseph's brothers, who sold him into slavery. Between the time of Joseph and the time of Moses, the pharaohs turned against Israel. The psalmist does not hesitate to attribute the Egyptians' hatred to God:

> The LORD made his people very fruitful;
> he made them too numerous for their foes,
> whose hearts he turned to hate his people,
> to conspire against his servants. (Ps. 105:24)

When God spoke with Moses about delivering Israel from Egypt, he told him in advance that Pharaoh would not let Israel go unless he was compelled by "a mighty hand" (Ex. 3:19). Then God hardened the heart of Pharaoh to create that unwillingness (4:21; 7:3, 13; 9:12; 10:1, 20, 27; 11:10; 14:4, 8).[13] Note the sustained emphasis on God's agency. It is also true that Pharaoh hardened his own heart (8:15), but in the narrative God's hardening of him is clearly prior and receives greater emphasis. To harden one's heart is to refuse God's commands, even refusing to listen to them or take them seriously. Clearly it is a sin. God warns against it (see Ps. 95:7–8). But in this case God made it happen, for his own specific purpose (Rom. 9:17). Having discussed God's dealings with Pharaoh, Paul summarizes: "Therefore God has mercy on whom he wants to have mercy, and he hardens whom he wants to harden" (Rom. 9:18).

No doubt Pharaoh was a wicked man before this time, and God's hardening of him could be seen from a human point of view as a natural extension of Pharaoh's previous attitudes, or even as a divine punishment for previous sin. (When we probe more deeply, however, we have to ask, in the light of the rest of Scripture, how God was previously

---

13. Compare Ex. 14:17–18, where God hardens the hearts of the Egyptian soldiers, so that they might know that he is Yahweh.

involved with Pharaoh's heredity, environment, character, and decisions.) That is true of all the hardening passages in Scripture; God doesn't harden people who have been good and faithful to him. Nevertheless, the hardening comes from God. He does deal with sinners by causing them to become more sinful.[14]

Pharaoh is not the only example, by any means. Frequently in Scripture, we read of God hardening hearts. Sihon, king of Heshbon, would not allow Israel to pass through his land on the way to Canaan, because "the LORD your God has made his spirit stubborn and his heart obstinate in order to give him into your hands, as he has now done" (Deut. 2:30; cf. Josh. 11:18–20; 1 Sam. 2:25; 2 Chron. 25:20). Similarly, God sent "an evil spirit" upon Saul to torment him (1 Sam. 16:14). Later, God sent another spirit, who caused the false prophets to lie, in order to lead wicked King Ahab to the battle in which he would die (1 Kings 22:20–23).[15]

God hardened the people of Israel as well as their evil kings. He gave Isaiah a prophetic word, not to bless, but to harden the people. God told him:

> Make the heart of this people calloused;
>   make their ears dull
>   and close their eyes.
> Otherwise they might see with their eyes,
>   hear with their ears,
>   understand with their hearts,
> and turn and be healed. (Isa. 6:10)

---

14. Rom. 1:24–32 describes how God gave sinners over to their lusts, so that they would commit greater sins.

15. On the theme of God sending evil or deceitful spirits, see Judg. 9:23 and 2 Kings 19:5–7. In 2 Thess. 2:11–12, we are told that before the coming of Christ, Satan will work counterfeit miracles, and "God sends them a powerful delusion so that they will believe the lie and so that all will be condemned who have not believed the truth but have delighted in wickedness."

Later, Isaiah asks,

> Why, O Lord, do you make us wander from your ways
> and harden our hearts so we do not revere you?
> (Isa. 63:17)

Then he complains,

> No one calls on your name
> or strives to lay hold of you;
> for you have hidden your face from us
> and made us waste away because of our sins.
> (Isa. 64:7)

Other nations, too, are objects of God's hardening. His prophets sometimes foretell that nations and individuals will rebel against God. As we have seen, Isaiah prophesies that God will send the Assyrians to plunder and trample Israel (10:5–11). The Assyrian comes to do vile things, but he comes, says God, because "I send him" (v. 6). Similarly, Gog will sinfully attack God's people, "so that the nations may know me when I show myself holy through you before their eyes" (Ezek. 38:16). The prophecy indicates God's purpose: to bring about the sin of the people, in order to glorify himself in the way he deals with it.

Sometimes, without mention of prophecy, Scripture indicates that God brought about a sinful action. Samson sought out a Philistine woman to be his wife, although God had forbidden his people to marry people from the surrounding nations. His parents were properly indignant, but they "did not know that this was from the Lord, who was seeking an occasion to confront the Philistines" (Judg. 14:4). Similarly, in 2 Samuel 24, the Lord incites David to conduct a census, for which God later judges him and for which David repents.

Several times in the Old Testament, God prevents certain people from following wise counsel. Absalom, the rebellious son of David, would not listen to the wise counselor Ahithophel, "for the LORD had determined to frustrate the good advice of Ahithophel in order to bring disaster on Absalom" (2 Sam. 17:14). Later, King Solomon's son and successor, Rehoboam, also ignored wise counselors and the pleas of the people, and sought to establish himself as a fearsome despot, which led to the secession of the northern tribes. He did not listen to wiser men "for this turn of events was from the LORD, to fulfill the word the LORD had spoken to Jeroboam son of Nebat through Ahijah the Shilonite" (1 Kings 12:15). God also prevented Amaziah, king of Judah, from obeying wise counsel, since he intended to bring judgment on him (2 Chron. 25:20).

Moving to the New Testament, we find that Jesus quotes Isaiah 6 in Matthew 13:14–15 to explain why he uses parables: to enlighten the disciples, but also to harden the wicked. This passage is also mentioned in John 12:40 to explain why the Jews disbelieved despite miraculous signs. Jesus also mentions sinful actions necessitated by prophecy. In John 13:18 (quoting Ps. 41:9), he excludes his betrayer from his blessing:

> I am not referring to all of you; I know those I have chosen. But this is to fulfill the scripture: "He who shares my bread has lifted up his heel against me."

Jesus knows who the betrayer is before the betrayal. He indicates that God, through Scripture, has made betrayal necessary. In John 15:25, Jesus explains why the Jews unreasonably disbelieved in him despite many signs and wonders: "This is to fulfill what is written in their Law: 'They hated me without reason.'"

Paul speaks of the apostles' ministry in the same way as Isaiah 6 (2 Cor. 2:15–16), as does Peter (1 Peter 2:6–8).[16] In

16. Peter adds that the unbelievers "were destined for" disobedience.

Scripture. God's word typically brings light and salvation. But in some cases, it brings hardening: darkness and unbelief.

Paul regards God's hardening as the reason for the unbelief of the Jews (Rom. 11:7–8, alluding to Isa. 29:10). He argues in the context (chapters 9–11) that God had to bring about the unbelief of Israel in order to accomplish the ingathering of the Gentiles (see 9:22–26 and 11:11–16, 25–32, followed by Paul's great hymn to the incomprehensible purposes of God).

Preceding Israel's hardening, however, was God's hardening of the Gentiles. God had revealed himself plainly to all nations through the creation (Rom. 1:19–20), but the nations had rejected God's revelation, refusing to glorify him, worshiping idols, and exchanging the truth for a lie (vv. 21–25). God's response was to harden them:

> Therefore God gave them over in the sinful desires of their hearts to sexual impurity. . . . Because of this, God gave them over to shameful lusts. . . . He gave them over to a depraved mind. (vv. 24–28)

God's sovereignty over human sin culminates in his foreordination of what John Murray called "the arch crime of history," the murder of the Son of God. As we have seen, Judas's betrayal,[17] the Jews' murderous hatred of Jesus, and the horrible injustice of the Romans, were all due to "God's set purpose and foreknowledge" (Acts 2:23). These people did what God's "power and will had decided beforehand should happen" (Acts 4:28; cf. 13:27; Luke 22:22). The crucifixion of Jesus could not have happened without sin, for Jesus did not deserve death. For God to foreordain the Crucifixion, he had to foreordain sinful actions to bring it about.

Finally, in the book of Revelation, when the evil beast sets up his satanic rule among the nations of the world, we read

---

17. The parallel with Joseph's betrayal by his brothers is significant.

that "God has put it into their hearts to accomplish his purpose by agreeing to give the beast their power to rule, until God's words are fulfilled" (17:17).

In summary, the teacher of wisdom says,

> The LORD works out everything for his own ends—
> even the wicked for a day of disaster. (Prov. 16:4)[18]

Faith and Salvation

In some ways, this section will be much happier than the last, for it deals with the positive side of God's sovereignty, rather than the negative. But we should remember that the two sides are quite inseparable; they reinforce one another. If saving faith is a gift of God, then the lack of saving faith, sinful unbelief, comes from God's withholding of that blessing.[19] Thus, this section will reinforce the previous one.

Nevertheless, we should rejoice that "salvation comes from the LORD" (Jonah 2:9). We saw in our discussion of the history of redemption that God sovereignly rescues his people from sin and its consequences. Without God's salvation, we were all once without hope, "dead in [our] transgressions and sins" (Eph. 2:1), "by nature objects of wrath" (2:3). But, says Paul,

> because of his great love for us, God, who is rich in mercy, made us alive with Christ even when we were dead in transgressions—it is by grace you have been saved. And God raised us up with Christ and seated us with him in the

---

18. As often in Scripture, this verse about God's control of wickedness precedes another verse that emphasizes the responsibility of the wicked for their own actions: "The LORD detests all the proud of heart. Be sure of this: They will not go unpunished" (v. 5).

19. Note Deut. 29:4, "But to this day the LORD has not given you a mind that understands or eyes that see or ears that hear."

No Other God

If salvation is strictly a work of God then He foreordained it, thus He foreknew it.

heavenly realms in Christ Jesus, in order that in the coming ages he might show the incomparable riches of his grace, expressed in his kindness to us in Christ Jesus. For it is by grace you have been saved, through faith—and this not from yourselves, it is the gift of God—not by works, so that no one can boast. For we are God's workmanship, created in Christ Jesus to do good works, which God prepared in advance for us to do. (Eph. 2:4–10)

This means the two are tied to by God's providence

This is the gospel, the central message of Scripture, that God came in Christ to reconcile us to himself by grace—by God's unmerited favor to those who deserve wrath. As we see, grace is opposed to works. Salvation comes, not through what we do, but through what God does for us. We have nothing to boast about. We are guilty sinners, whose only hope is God's mercy.

So salvation is God's work—not only in its broad historical outlines, as we saw earlier, but also for each of us as individuals. It is an exercise of God's sovereign control over his world and his creatures. That control began before we were conceived—indeed, before the world was made. For Paul tells us that

[God] chose us in [Christ] before the creation of the world to be holy and blameless in his sight. In love he predestined us to be adopted as his sons through Jesus Christ, in accordance with his pleasure and will—to the praise of his glorious grace, which he has freely given us in the One he loves. (Eph. 1:4–6; cf. 2 Tim. 1:9)

Here we learn of God's choice (*election* is the theological term) of a people for himself, before the foundation of the world. Salvation is ultimately by divine appointment, divine choice (cf. Acts 13:48; 1 Thess. 1:4; 5:9; 2 Thess. 2:13–14).

Certainly there is also a human choice, a choice to receive Christ, to believe in him (John 1:12; 3:15–16; 6:29, 40;

11:26).[20] Without this choice, there is no salvation (John 3:36). There are also human decisions to follow Jesus, to obey his commandments—decisions that Scripture continually urges us to make (e.g., John 14:15, 21, 23). But which choice comes first? Does God choose us for salvation and then move us to respond, or do we first choose him and thereby motivate him to choose us for salvation?

The second alternative is quite impossible, since it violates the very idea of grace. If our choosing of God moves him to save us, then salvation is based on a work of ours, and we have something to boast about.[21]

Furthermore, God's choosing took place in eternity past, before anyone was even conceived. Before we began to exist, God's plan for us was fully formulated. We can no more change God's decision than we can change our grandparents.

Arminian theology, nevertheless, asserts that God chooses us because he knows in advance that we will choose to believe in him. On this view, our choice is the cause, and God's choice is the effect. We are the first cause, and God is the second. Some have supported this understanding by appealing to Romans 8:29 and 1 Peter 1:2, which say that election is based on "foreknowledge." But the foreknowledge in these passages is not God's foreknowledge that we will choose him.

20. Some Calvinists have used John 15:16, "You did not choose me, but I chose you," to prove that there is no human choice at all. That claim is, of course, nonsense in the light of the many passages that indicate the importance of human decision in our relationship to Jesus. In John 15:16, Jesus is not saying that the disciples made no decision to follow him; rather, he is indicating that his choice, not theirs, marked the beginning of their relationship to him as disciples and apostles.

21. The response of Arminians and others is to deny that faith is a work. It is true that faith has no merit that would move God to save us. That is true of anything and everything we do. But the Arminian wants to have it both ways. He wants to say that faith has no merit, but he also wants to say that our faith somehow motivates God to save us, that God chooses us on the basis of our choosing him. But if our faith motivates God to save us, then it must have merit in his eyes.

No Other God

Often in the biblical languages, as in English, when the verb *know* has a noun rather than a fact-clause as its object,[22] it refers to a personal relationship, not a knowledge of information. In Psalm 1:6, for example, we learn that "the LORD watches over [Heb. *knows*] the way of the righteous." This does not simply mean that God knows what the righteous are doing, which would be rather obvious, but that he guards and keeps them. Compare Amos 3:2:

> You only have I chosen [Heb. *known*]
>   of all the families of the earth;
> therefore I will punish you
>   for all your sins.

The NIV's translation, "chosen," is correct. God is not confessing ignorance of all the families of the earth other than Israel. Rather, he is claiming a special covenant relationship with Israel, a covenant that in context they have broken. Compare Hos. 13:4; Matt. 25:12; John 10:14; Rom. 11:2 ("foreknew"); 1 Cor. 8:3; 1 Thess. 5:12 (where *know* is translated "respect"); 1 Peter 1:20 (where *foreknown* is again translated "chosen"). So in Romans 8:29, when Paul says that God "foreknew" believers, this means that he established a personal relationship with them (from all eternity, according to Ephesians 1:4–5). The Greek word translated "foreknew" could also be translated "befriended," "foreloved," or even "chose" or "elected."[23]

---

22. This is the difference between "knowing him" and "knowing that." For example, consider the difference between "I know Bill" and "I know that Bill is forty-three years old."

23. It is interesting to note that open theist Gregory A. Boyd, having rejected the doctrine of God's exhaustive foreknowledge, actually adopts the traditional Calvinistic interpretation of Rom. 8:29, seeing in it a personal knowledge, rather than a knowledge of future facts (*God of the Possible* [Grand Rapids: Baker, 2000], 47–48). However, he sees a reference here to God's election of corporate entities, not individuals. On that issue, see chapter 6 of this book.

The open-theist view is even further from the biblical teaching than the Arminian view. For the open theist denies even that God knows in advance who will and will not believe. So the open theist can make no sense at all of biblical passages dealing with the election of individuals to salvation before the foundation of the world.

So Scripture teaches all believers, as Jesus taught his disciples, "You did not choose me, but I chose you and appointed you to go and bear fruit—fruit that will last" (John 15:16). God's choice precedes our choice, our response, our faith. How could it be otherwise, considering everything we have already observed about God's sovereignty throughout nature, history, and human life in general? Can the choice to believe in Christ be the one choice that is beyond God's control? Is salvation the one area in which we should *not* give God the praise? [24]

Many passages explicitly teach that our response is God's gift. Jesus teaches that "all that the Father gives me will come to me" (John 6:37), that "no one can come to me unless the Father who sent me draws him, and I will raise him up at the last day" (6:44), [25] and that "no one can come to me unless the Father has enabled him" (6:65). It is only by the Spirit that we call upon God as *Abba*, Father (Rom. 8:15).

When Paul and Silas first brought the gospel to the city of Philippi, one of their listeners was a woman named Lydia. "The Lord opened her heart to respond to Paul's message," whereupon she and her household were baptized (Acts 16:14–15). This language is quite straightforward: her faith

24. Thanks to Vern Poythress for suggesting to me this profound question.
25. "Draw" (*helko*) is a strong word, sometimes translated "drag." The one dragged may resist, but not successfully. See John 18:10; 21:6, 11; Acts 16:19; 21:30; James 2:6. Arminian theologians point out that in John 12:32 Jesus promises to "draw all men" to himself. Here, too, the drawing is efficacious. But in context (especially vv. 20–22), he is promising to draw people of all nations, not only Jews—a regular theme in John's gospel (1:13; 10:16; 11:51). So in John 12:32, Jesus is not promising to draw every single human being to himself.

came from God. Earlier, in Pisidian Antioch, a number of Gentiles came to faith in Christ, and "all who were appointed for eternal life believed" (13:48).[26] The divine appointment came first; belief (faith) was the result.[27] Therefore, people believe when God's hand is with the apostles (11:21); their conversion is evidence of God's grace (v. 23). In 18:27, also, converts are those "who by grace had believed." (Compare Rom. 12:3; 1 Cor. 2:5; 12:9; Eph. 6:23; Phil. 1:29; 1 Thess. 1:4–5.)

Repentance, too, is the work of God in us. It is the opposite side of faith. Faith is turning to Christ; repentance is turning away from sin. You cannot have one without the other. As with faith, it is God who grants repentance. We noticed earlier that God sometimes hardens hearts, in effect keeping them from repentance. God also acts positively to give the spirit of repentance. In a passage that vividly anticipates the sufferings of Christ, God announces through Zechariah:

> I will pour out on the house of David and the inhabitants of Jerusalem a spirit of grace and supplication. They will look on me, the one they have pierced, and they will mourn for him as one mourns for an only child, and grieve bitterly for him as one grieves for a firstborn son. (Zech. 12:10)

So Jesus is exalted from the cross to God's right hand "as Prince and Savior that he might give repentance and forgive-

---

26. This principle throws light on John 10:26, where Jesus tells the Jews, "You do not believe because you are not my sheep." To be Jesus' sheep is to be elect, to be appointed for eternal life. "I give them eternal life, and they shall never perish; no one can snatch them out of my hand" (v. 28). Again, election precedes believing. Note the same relationship in John 17, where Jesus speaks of his disciples as those whom the Father has given to him (vv. 2, 6). He tells the Father that he has taught these elect people, and as a result they have believed (vv. 6–8).

27. Thus, God tells Paul to remain at Corinth, despite persecution, "because I have many people in this city" (Acts 18:10). God is not speaking of people who have already believed, but of those who will believe through Paul's one-and-a-half-year ministry there. The people already belong to God because of their election, and they will come to believe through Paul's preaching.

---

ness of sins to Israel" (Acts 5:31). Later, Jewish Christians give thanks that "God has granted even the Gentiles repentance unto life" (11:18; cf. also 2 Tim. 2:25).

Many biblical teachings underscore the sovereignty of God in salvation. We will not be able to look at them in detail, but I should mention them. There is the doctrine of effectual calling, by which God efficaciously summons people into union with Christ (Rom. 1:6–7; 8:30; 11:29; 1 Cor. 1:2, 9, 24, 26; 2 Thess. 2:13–14; Heb. 3:1; 2 Peter 1:10). *Calling* does not always refer to effectual calling; it does not in Matthew 22:14 (and 20:16 KJV), where "many are invited [Gr. *called*], but few are chosen." Here the word refers to the universal offer of salvation through Christ, an offer that many refuse. But in the passages mentioned earlier, the "called" are those whom God has sovereignly brought from death to life.

There is also the doctrine of regeneration, the new birth. The new birth, like effectual calling, is an act of God, not something that we can bring about.[28] In the classic passage, John 3, Jesus tells Nicodemus that to be born again is to be born by the Spirit of God (vv. 5–6). In bringing about the new birth, the Spirit works as he pleases, invisibly, like the wind (v. 8).[29] How is the new birth a birth? It is the beginning of new spiritual life. We recall Paul telling us that by nature we are "dead in [our] transgressions and sins" (Eph. 2:1). The new birth brings life out of that death. Without this new birth, we cannot even see the kingdom of God (John 3:3), because our spiritual eyes are dead. Paul teaches in Romans 1 that sinners suppress the truth and exchange it for a lie. So the new birth marks the beginning of spiritual understanding, as well as the beginning of obedient discipleship.

28. This is part of the thrust of the birth metaphor. Clearly, we had no part in bringing about our physical birth. Our physical life came from others. Similarly, spiritual life comes from another, by divine grace.

29. Other passages emphasizing divine sovereignty in regeneration are John 1:13; 1 John 2:29; 3:9; 4:7; 5:1, 4, 18.

Other passages also emphasize that our spiritual understanding is a gift of God. In Matthew 11:25–27, we learn that God the Father and God the Son both hide spiritual insight from some and reveal it to others. "No one knows the Father," says Jesus, "except the Son and those to whom the Son chooses to reveal him." John tells us that "the Son of God has come and has given us understanding" (1 John 5:20); compare his words about the anointing of the Spirit (2:20–21, 27). Paul talks about the wisdom of Christ, hidden for a time, "that God destined for our glory before time began" (1 Cor. 2:7). He goes on to say that no one can understand the wisdom of Christ without God's Spirit (vv. 12–16). And when Paul speaks about the power of his preaching to bring faith, he regularly ascribes that persuasive power to God's Spirit (1 Cor. 2:4–5; 1 Thess. 1:5; 2 Thess. 2:14).[30] Unless God has given us a mind to understand, we will not appreciate his message (Deut. 29:4; cf. Isa. 6:9–10, discussed previously). So we ask God for wisdom, knowing that for Jesus' sake he is willing to give it, and that he is the only ultimate source of spiritual knowledge (James 1:5; cf. Eph. 1:17–19; Col. 1:9).[31]

Scripture also employs other ways of describing how God brings us from death and ignorance to life and spiritual perception. God circumcises our heart (Deut. 30:6), writes his law on our heart (Jer. 31:31–34), gives us a new heart (Ezek. 11:19; 36:26), gives us a heart to know him (Jer. 24:7), washes

L?desire

30. On the internal testimony of the Spirit, see John Murray, "The Attestation of Scripture," in *The Infallible Word*, ed. N. B. Stonehouse and Paul Woolley (Grand Rapids: Eerdmans, 1946), 40–52; John M. Frame, "The Spirit and the Scriptures," in *Hermeneutics, Authority, and Canon*, ed. D. A. Carson and John D. Woodbridge (Grand Rapids: Zondervan, 1986).

31. So knowledge of God is part of the new life in Christ. It is not merely intellectual; its intellectual aspect is part of an overall covenantal arrangement. "The fear of the LORD is the beginning of wisdom" (Ps. 111:10; cf. Deut. 4:6; Prov. 1:7; 9:10; 15:33; Isa. 33:6). See my *The Doctrine of the Knowledge of God* (Phillipsburg, N.J.: Presbyterian and Reformed, 1987) for the implications of this for the Christian theory of knowledge.

and renews us (Titus 3:4–7), creates us anew (2 Cor. 5:17), shines his light into our darkness (2 Cor. 4:6),[32] raises us from the dead with Christ to new life (Rom. 6:4), and begins a good work in us (Phil. 1:6). These expressions do not always refer to initial regeneration, the very beginnings of spiritual life, but they do refer to our spiritual life and knowledge as the work of God.

So our continuing life with God is like its beginning: we are constantly dependent on the Lord for the resources to live obediently. Without him, we can do nothing (John 15:5). We saw earlier that God is sovereign over the free decisions of people, including decisions to commit sin. And in the outworkings of saving grace, it is God who motivates his people to obey him. Sanctification, as well as regeneration, is his work, although of course we are responsible for what we do.

So we recall Ephesians 2, where verse 10 teaches, "We are God's workmanship, created in Christ Jesus to do good works, which God prepared in advance for us to do." We know that without God's grace, we are dead in sin (v. 1; Rom. 7:18; 8:6–8). We cannot do anything good on our own. So as we work out our salvation, we know that "it is God who works in you to will and to act according to his good pleasure" (Phil. 2:13). It is the Lord who sanctifies, who makes his people holy (Lev. 20:8). He is the one who makes his people willing to work for him (Hag. 1:14), who stirs them up to generous giving and devotion to the Lord's work (1 Chron. 29:14–19; cf. 1 Kings 8:5–8). Although we are not sinlessly perfect in this life (1 John 1:8–10), he is working to perfect in us the image of Christ (Jer. 32:39–40; Eph. 5:25–27). So we pray that God will enable us to please him, for we know that that is his will, and that only he can make that happen (Col. 1:10–12).

---

32. Paul here draws a parallel to the creation of light in Gen. 1:3. There is light, when before there was only darkness.

God is also the source of any success we may have in proclaiming his word. Paul admits that his confidence in his ministry is not based on anything in him: "Not that we are competent in ourselves to claim anything for ourselves, but our competence comes from God" (2 Cor. 3:5). And "we have this treasure in jars of clay to show that this all-surpassing power is from God and not from us" (4:7; cf. 10:17). God uses us to minister to others, by means of his gifts (Rom. 12:3–8; 1 Cor. 4:7; 12:1–11; Eph. 4:1–13). These passages emphasize over and over that these are gifts of God, in Christ, by the Spirit.

So God's grace is the source of every blessing that we have as Christians. Truly, as Jesus said, "apart from me you can do nothing" (John 15:5). We have nothing that we have not received (1 Cor. 4:7). Even our response to his grace is given by grace. When God saves us, he takes away every possible ground of boasting (Eph. 2:9; 1 Cor. 1:29). All the praise and glory belongs to him.

Summary Passages

I do not apologize for including such a large number of Scripture passages in this chapter. Nothing is more important, especially at this point in the history of theology, than for God's people to be firmly convinced that Scripture teaches God's universal control over the world, and teaches it over and over again. Scripture mentions and implies this control in many different historical and doctrinal contexts and applies it to our own life with God in a great number of ways. This sheer quantity and variety of teaching on the subject is a major point of this chapter.

I have listed these passages with little comment, for they speak for themselves. It ought to be evident now that even if there are interpretive difficulties in some of these passages, it is quite impossible to escape the cumulative force of all of them. As B. B. Warfield said with regard to biblical inspiration, the total evidence for it is like an all-devouring avalanche. One may deftly avoid a few rocks, but one cannot escape them all.

This pervasive scriptural witness sets the context in which we should consider the relatively few passages that explicitly state that God controls everything that comes to pass. In view of what we have seen, we should not expect these passages to be limited in their application. We have already shown that everything that happens in this world—both major events and tiny details—is under God's sovereign control. The passages that explicitly teach universal foreordination only summarize, with the helpful redundancy that is characteristic of Scripture, this large quantity of biblical data.

Let us now look at four passages that explicitly teach the universality of God's control over the world. First, let us note Lamentations 3:37–38:

> Who can speak and have it happen
>   if the Lord has not decreed it?
> Is it not from the mouth of the Most High
>   that both calamities and good things come?

Here the scope of God's decree is said to be universal: it covers all calamities and all good things. Nobody can make anything happen unless God has decreed that it will happen.

Next, observe what Paul teaches in Romans 8:28:

> And we know that in all things God works for the good of those who love him, who have been called according to his purpose.

Paul has been talking about the sufferings that Christians must endure in hope of the glory to come. These sufferings have a cosmic dimension: "The whole creation has been groaning as in the pains of childbirth right up to the present time" (v. 22). In view, therefore, are not only persecutions for the sake of Christ, but all the sufferings introduced into the creation by the fall of Adam: the pain of childbirth and the thorns and thistles in the world (Gen. 3:14–19). These sufferings "are not worth comparing with the glory that will be revealed in us" (Rom. 8:18), but for the moment they are difficult to bear. The good news is that Jesus' atonement has cosmic dimensions: in time it will counteract all the effects of the Fall, as well as sin itself, so that "the creation itself will be liberated from its bondage to decay and brought into the glorious freedom of the children of God" (v. 21). Therefore, God is now working in all things, not only when we suffer for the gospel, to bring about good for those who have been effectually called into fellowship with Christ. For our purposes, the conclusion is that every event is part of God's great plan to richly bless his people. We often do not see how the sufferings of this world will enhance the joy to come, but we trust that God is bringing about that result, since he works in, and therefore controls, all things.

This confidence that God is working in *all things* leads to a great hymn of confidence, which ends,

> For I am convinced that neither death nor life, neither angels nor demons, neither the present nor the future, nor any powers, neither height nor depth, nor anything else in all creation, will be able to separate us from the love of God that is in Christ Jesus our Lord. (vv. 38–39)

Let us look now at Ephesians 1:11, which reads,

> In [Christ] we were also chosen, having been predestined according to the plan of him who works out everything in conformity with the purpose of his will.

This is not the first reference in this chapter to God's sovereign predestination. Verse 4 mentions election, and verse 5 mentions predestination to adoption as sons. The first part of verse 11 ("chosen," "predestined") recapitulates the teaching of the earlier verses. But the reference to "the plan of him who works out everything" must go beyond that recapitulation. It is unlikely that Paul would have said repetitively that we have been elected and predestined according to the plan of him who elects and predestines. Rather, Paul is saying that God's saving election and predestination are part of a larger program. Salvation is part of God's overall control of the world he has made. Salvation will certainly be consummated, because the Savior is the one who controls all things.

Finally, we return to Romans. Paul teaches in Romans 9–11 that God has hardened the hearts of many Jews, in order to open the door of blessing to Gentiles. After all that is said, much remains mysterious. Paul's response is not to question God's fairness or love. He answers such complaints with the analogy of the potter and the clay (9:21–24): what right has the clay to question the prerogatives of the potter?[33] But obviously much mystery remains. Overwhelmed, Paul praises God's very incomprehensibility:

> Oh, the depth of the riches of the wisdom and knowledge
>   of God!
>   How unsearchable his judgments,
>   and his paths beyond tracing out!
> "Who has known the mind of the Lord?
>   Or who has been his counselor?"

33. Boyd, in *God of the Possible,* 141, suggests that in Jer. 18 and Rom. 9 the clay resists the potter's intentions, forcing him to revise his plans. But Paul's specific point is that the clay *cannot* resist the potter's will—hence the question in Rom. 9:19. The issue in Jer. 18 and Rom. 9:19–21 is not whether the potter controls the clay, but whether he has *the right* to control the clay in such a way. And, of course, the answer is yes. For Sanders's discussion of the potter passages, see chapter 8.

"Who has ever given to God,
   that God should repay him?"
For from him and through him and to him are all things.
   To him be the glory forever! Amen. (11:33–36,
      quoting Isa. 40:13 and Job 41:11)

Verse 36 ascribes everything in creation to God. These "things" are not just material objects, but also events: the "judgments" and "paths" of verse 33, including God's judgment of Israel and his blessing of the Gentiles. God's involvement with his world is threefold: as its creator ("from him"), its governor ("through him"), and the ultimate purpose ("unto him") of the whole world. God controls all things.

Incredibly, neither Sanders's *The God Who Risks* nor Boyd's *God of the Possible* lists Ephesians 1:11 in the Scripture index. Boyd doesn't list Romans 11:36 or Lamentations 3:37–38, either. Sanders discusses the general contexts of the Romans and Lamentations passages, but he does not mention the indications there of the universality of God's controlling plan. At the very least, it seems that the open theists are not dealing seriously with the strongest biblical evidence against their position.[34] But even apart from these explicitly universal texts, there is surely enough biblical data for us to conclude that God's sovereign control extends to everything.

---

34. In the open-theist literature, there is a general failure to interact with significant Scripture passages used by the other side. Roger Nicole points out that Boyd's *God of the Possible* "contains no reference to any of the 26 passages in which the words 'elect' or 'election' are found, except Rom. 8:33, 9:11, and 11:28" ("A Review Article: God of the Possible?" *Reformation and Revival* 10, no. 1 [winter, 2001], 170–71). Nicole also notes that Boyd mentions only four of the nine passages dealing with God's purpose before creation, and only five of the eighty-nine passages "in which God is presented as the one who chooses those on whom he will bestow his blessing."

How Do Open Theists Reply?

In the previous chapter, I likened the biblical references to God's exhaustive foreordination to an avalanche: there may be interpretive problems in this or that text, but the doctrine is so pervasive in Scripture that no one can escape its cumulative force. Nevertheless, open theists (like Arminians, Socinians, Molinists, and Pelagians before them) deny this teaching. In this chapter, I shall examine some of their objections to it, leaving a few others to later chapters.

Universalizing Particulars?

Sanders agrees with Fredrik Lindström[1] that "the basic problem . . . is that commentators rush to assert a universal principle instead of placing the texts in their literary and historical contexts."[2] Here is Sanders's treatment of one text as an example of the argument he applies to others:

---

1. Sanders cites Fredrik Lindström, *God and the Origin of Evil: A Contextual Analysis of Alleged Monistic Evidence in the Old Testament* (Lund: CWK Gleerup, 1983).

2. John Sanders, *The God Who Risks* (Downers Grove, Ill.: InterVarsity Press, 1998), 82.

Isaiah 45:7 states, "I form light and create darkness, I make weal and create woe; I the LORD do all these things." Does this mean that God is responsible for every single act of good and evil in the entire cosmos? Not at all, for as Lindström observes, the entire section pertains to Yahweh's dealings with Israel, not the entire cosmos. This is evidenced by the terms used. "Light" (*'or*) is not used in Isaiah 40–55 to refer to cosmic creation. Rather, it is used as a metaphor for political liberation from the Babylonians (Isa. 42:6; 49:6; 53:11). The same is true of "darkness" (*hosek*), which is a metaphor for misfortune and captivity (42:7; 47:5; 49:9).[3]

Certainly liberation from the Babylonian exile is a general concern of Isaiah 40–66. But not one of the passages on Sanders's list, with the possible exception of 49:9, uses *light* primarily as a metaphor for political deliverance or *darkness* as a metaphor for captivity. In Isaiah 42:6 and 49:6, God calls his servant "a light for the Gentiles." Does this mean that he is the political deliverer of the Gentiles from Babylonian captivity? That exegesis makes little sense. And does Sanders really want to restrict the meaning of 53:11 so that the messianic Servant, after his sufferings, will see deliverance from political captivity?

In the context, it makes much more sense to interpret "light" in 45:7 as an allusion to Genesis 1. God has made the earth (vv. 12, 18), and he has made Israel (vv. 10–11). As the potter has the right to do as he wishes with his clay, so God will do whatever he wills with his people (vv. 9–11). The heavens will rain down righteousness, and the earth will bring forth salvation (v. 8), just as God caused the plants to grow in Genesis. Clearly, then, the "light" and "darkness" of verse 7 allude to the original creation, in which God made literal light and literal darkness.

3. Ibid.

Symbolically, as in Scripture generally, "light" refers to God's glory, and therefore to his presence, particularly his presence in blessing. To dwell in light, then, is to dwell in his presence, and that presence can be taken cultically (being proximate to the temple) or ethically (reflecting his righteousness). "Light" is therefore a fitting metaphor for deliverance from political exile, since the Jewish captives return to the land of God's presence. But its political significance does not exhaust its meaning. Rather, the term has political significance because it has a wider theological significance.

That significance is important in the context of 45:7. God is speaking to Cyrus, the Persian emperor,[4] promising that he, the Lord, will give Cyrus victory over all his adversaries. He can do this because he is the Creator of all (v. 12). Nobody can give orders to him or demand answers from him (v. 11). He is the potter; we are the clay (vv. 9–11). As he sends rain to make things grow (v. 8), so he will send righteousness as a rain upon the earth. Because of his sovereignty over all things, he is able to overcome all obstacles to Cyrus's hegemony (vv. 1–6). Political deliverance for Israel is one result of these divine acts, but the more important result is "that from the rising of the sun to the place of its setting men may know there is none besides me. I am the LORD, and there is no other" (v. 6).

So "form the light" in 45:7 does not refer merely to political deliverance. The use of *light* in these chapters and the emphasis of God's address to Cyrus suggest, rather, that God's sovereignty over light and darkness (taken in both literal and symbolic senses) is the *ground* for his political deliverance. Cyrus should expect God to deliver Israel, because God is

4. On a conservative chronology, God here speaks to Cyrus several centuries before his birth, which strengthens the case for an emphasis here on God's radical sovereignty.

sovereign over everything, as he demonstrates in creation, providence, and Cyrus's own conquests.

Every passage of Scripture, of course, refers in some way to a specific situation in time and space. But Scripture always interprets such specific situations in the light of eternal and universal principles. So here, Cyrus's political success is based on the universal sovereignty of God. It is often tempting to limit the meaning of a text to a narrow context, especially when we are biased against the implications of a broader interpretation. But the fact that a text addresses a specific context never rules out the possibility that it also teaches principles of broad, even universal, extension. Indeed, biblical writers typically address particular situations by appealing to principles that apply to many situations beyond the immediate context. Therefore, we should be careful about relating universals to particulars. In this sort of exegetical issue, it is all too easy to succumb to theological bias. We should remember that particularizing universals is at least as bad as universalizing particulars.

In Isaiah 45:7, there is no reason to think that political deliverance exhausts the meaning of "light," and there is good reason in the context to believe that the ground of the political deliverance is God's universal sovereignty. Besides, as I demonstrated in the previous chapter, many other passages declare that God alone is the ultimate source of prosperity and disaster, of weal and woe.

Sanders also complains when he finds Calvin reasoning from particulars to generalities: from texts in which God sends wind and rain in particular situations to the general assertion that all wind and rain come from God.[5] But, as we saw in the previous chapter, the Psalms are full of the teaching that God directs the weather in general. To the psalmists,

5. Sanders, *The God Who Risks*, 81.

the notion that God only sometimes controls the wind and rain would be absurd.

The sheer number and weight of the passages we discussed in chapter 5 are sufficient to overcome Sanders's objection. Scripture does often speak of God governing specific situations. But it also speaks generally of God's sovereign control, in passages like Ephesians 1:11 and Romans 11:36 (passages that Sanders and Boyd barely mention), and it speaks specifically of his control in a vast number of particular cases. When the biblical writers speak of God's sovereign control in specific cases, that control comes as no surprise to them. For they are very much aware that God's specific actions are manifestations of his general sovereignty. They use no special criteria to distinguish between storms caused by God and others that have merely natural causes. Indeed, they know nothing of storms caused by merely natural causes. Rather, they ascribe storms to God because they know that all storms come from God.

Something should also be said about the implications of the notion that only *some* storms and other natural phenomena come from God. Open theists usually present God's self-limitation as an accommodation to human free will: God refuses to control human free choices, so there can be a "real relationship" between him and human beings. However, Sanders's view of the storms suggests something different—something even more extreme and more troubling. For the storms, after all, are not free agents. Why, then, should these natural phenomena be outside of God's control? The free-will arguments do not suffice to explain the independence of natural events from God's will. Is there some large element of chance or randomness in the universe with which God must contend? If so, one wonders whether, in the final analysis, God can achieve his purposes in such a universe. Are natural events caused by supernatural beings other than God? Such a notion suggests dualism or polytheism. Open theists certainly ought to get to work explaining how impersonal events escape God's sovereign control. To my knowledge, they have so far not attempted to explain it.

But I must return to the issue of universalizing particulars. In Daniel 2:38–40, God gives King Nebuchadnezzar a dream that describes the rise and fall of four successive empires reaching hundreds of years into the future. Gregory Boyd comments:

> The open view "explains" this and every other passage of Scripture that relates to the future by simply accepting that the future is settled to the extent that the passage in question says it is settled, no more or no less. . . . The open view does not read into these verses the *assumption* that the future must be exhaustively settled.[6]

Again, Boyd ignores passages like Ephesians 1:11 that warrant the very assumption he rejects. But apart from that, Boyd does not take seriously the vast context of events surrounding the rise and fall of empires. The fall of an empire is not a simple event. Empires fall because of weak leadership, military errors, internal governmental intrigue, indefensible borders, civil unrest, economic weakness, technological inferiority, moral and religious decline, and many other factors. And each of these factors is a complex pattern resulting from many other specific natural events and human decisions. The same is true for the rise of a rival empire. As we saw in the preceding chapter, God can hardly be said to control these large historical developments unless he also controls a vast number of smaller events.[7]

Daniel, the interpreter of the dream, sees the four empires as part of God's usual working: "He changes times and sea-

---

6. Gregory A. Boyd, *God of the Possible* (Grand Rapids: Baker, 2000), 42.
7. One is reminded of the poem about the battle that was lost "all for the want of a horseshoe nail."

sons; he sets up kings and deposes them" (Dan. 2:21). And in time, after some humiliation, even Nebuchadnezzar gets the message:

> His dominion is an eternal dominion;
>> his kingdom endures from generation to generation.
> All the peoples of the earth
>> are regarded as nothing.
> He does what he pleases
>> with the powers of heaven
>> and the peoples of the earth.
> No one can hold back his hand
>> or say to him, "What have you done?"
>>> (Dan. 4:34–35)

Is Nebuchadnezzar saying here that God does what he pleases only with *some* of the powers of heaven and *some* of the peoples of the earth? Certainly not. The "all" that begins verse 35 covers all the powers of heaven and all the peoples of the earth. To posit exceptions here would destroy the radical nature of the king's obeisance to Yahweh. Clearly the teaching of the book of Daniel is that God brings about *all* the movements of human history.

Divine Foreordination Versus Human Responsibility?

Another way that open theists challenge the thesis of universal divine foreordination is by drawing an antithesis between divine control and human free choice. Gregory Boyd, for example, denies the "deterministic" interpretation of Romans 9 because in verses 30–32 Paul says that blessing comes through faith. Boyd comments:

> Paul explains everything he's been talking about in this chapter by appealing to the morally responsible choices of the Israelites and Gentiles. . . . We see that God's process

of hardening some and having mercy on others is not arbitrary: God expresses "severity toward those who have fallen [the nation of Israel], but kindness toward you [believers], provided you continue in his kindness" (11:22).[8]

Romans 9–11 certainly does teach that both divine sovereignty and human responsibility are involved in God's saving work. It is important to understand the relationship between the two as clearly as we can, although some aspects of it are deeply mysterious. But we must not set them in opposition to one another. Boyd believes that the decision to exercise faith cannot be a morally responsible choice if faith is a gift of God. But in the previous chapter we noted a large number of passages that state that faith is a gift. So the references in 9:30–32 and 11:22 do not contradict the teaching of 9:15–18 that God has mercy on whom he will have mercy. Nor is God's decision of 9:15–18 subsequent to the human faith of 9:30–32, for the latter, as well as the former, is God's sovereign choice.

Boyd believes that human responsibility contradicts exhaustive divine foreordination because he believes that human responsibility depends on libertarian freedom. Later I shall argue that freedom in the libertarian sense is nonexistent, unscriptural, incoherent, and actually destructive of moral responsibility. If my position is correct, we must affirm both that God brings all things to pass and that human beings are morally responsible. These, I believe, are the consistent affirmations of Scripture.

What Kind of Election?

In chapter 5, I argued that in Scripture God chooses ("elects") people for salvation, and that his choice of them precedes their choice of him. Thus, God foreordains human

8. Boyd, *God of the Possible*, 140–41.

salvation, just as he foreordains everything else. Open theists do acknowledge that God chooses people for his purposes, but they insist that divine election is (1) primarily corporate, rather than individual, and (2) for service, rather than for salvation. Rice explains:

> Throughout the Bible divine election typically represents a corporate call to service. It applies to groups rather than to individuals, and it involves a role in God's saving work in the present world rather than in the future life (although this may be an extension of the former).[9]

Rice admits that in some cases God calls individuals as well as corporate groups, but he insists that "when God's call does focus on specific individuals, it represents a summons to service, not a guarantee of personal salvation."[10]

I agree that election in Scripture is not always individual and not always for salvation. We do need to make distinctions among the various meanings of *election* in various contexts. For example, Jesus chose Judas to be an apostle (John 6:70–71), but described him as a devil. In *The Doctrine of God,* I distinguish between historical and eternal election. In historical election, God chooses Abraham and his family to be a means of blessing to all nations (Gen. 12:1–3). But some of Abraham's family (Ishmael, Esau) do not receive the blessing of the covenant, nor do the unbelieving among the family of Israel (Rom. 9:1–13). The blessing, ultimately, is for the faithful remnant (Isa. 1:9; 10:20–22; 11:11, 16). But, in the final reckoning, nobody is faithful, except Jesus: he alone is the remnant, the elect. In the visible church, as in Israel, not all receive the ultimate blessing of the covenant. Some turn away from Jesus (John 6:66–67; Heb. 6:4–6; 10:26–31; 1 John

---

9. Richard Rice, "Biblical Support for a New Perspective," in OG, 56.
10. Ibid., 57.

2:19), but others receive salvation by virtue of their union with him.

So, in the historical sense, people can be elect and later nonelect. But Scripture also teaches a stronger kind of election that I describe as "eternal." In Ephesians 1:4, Paul says that God the Father "chose us in him [Jesus Christ] before the creation of the world to be holy and blameless in his sight." Here and in verses 5–14, it is clear that the outcome of God's election is salvation in the fullest sense: holiness, blamelessness, adoption as sons, the giving of redemptive grace, forgiveness, godly wisdom and understanding, faith, the Holy Spirit as a guarantee of inheritance, and the praise of God's glory. In Romans 8:30, Paul says that "those he predestined, he also called; those he called, he also justified; those he justified, he also glorified." Clearly, election in this sense results in salvation, and it cannot be lost, for its blessings are eternal.

Now Rice is right concerning historical election, but he ignores or denies the biblical teaching about eternal election. Historically, God does choose people for purposes other than to save them, although all these purposes are part of redemptive history. And in historical election, there is more of a focus on corporate groups than on individuals. But eternal election is different in these respects. Although it, too, deals with corporate groups, it is profoundly concerned with the individuals in those groups. In Romans 8:28–39 and Ephesians 1:3–14, for example, Paul discusses the election of individuals for salvation. It cannot be lost, and it leads to the fullness of divine blessing for all eternity. Restricting these passages to corporate groups takes the heart out of the profound, personal assurances to troubled saints that are found in them. The individual believer is the one who needs to know that no one can bring a charge against him (Rom. 8:33–34), and that no one can separate him from Jesus' love (vv. 35–39).

And it is the individual believer (together with other believers, to be sure) who is chosen to be holy and blameless in God's sight (Eph. 1:4), to be adopted as God's son (v. 4), to be redeemed (vv. 7–10), to hope in Christ (v. 12), and to be sealed with the Spirit (vv. 13–14). It is for these individuals, not for an abstract corporate unit, that Paul prays in verses 15–23 that they will have the Spirit of wisdom and revelation, enlightenment, hope, and divine power.

Scripture speaks of the election of individuals for salvation in many other passages, too. (See Matt. 24:22, 24, 31; Mark 13:20–22; Luke 18:7; Acts 13:48; 1 Cor. 1:27–28; Eph. 2:10; Col. 3:12; 1 Thess. 1:4–5; 2 Thess. 2:13; 2 Tim. 1:9; 2:10; Titus 1:1; James 2:5.)

Romans 9 should be added to this list, even though open theists think it deals with corporate election, rather than individual election. Sanders declares:

> Paul is not debating the eternal salvation and reprobation of individuals. . . . His concern, rather, is whether God's election of Israel has turned out to be a failure, since the majority of Jews were not accepting Jesus as the Messiah.[11]

Romans 9–11 does deal with corporate groups (Jews and Gentiles) and historical election. But it is also deeply concerned with the destinies of individuals. Paul begins by expressing "great sorrow and unceasing anguish in my heart" for his fellow Jews who have rejected Christ (9:2). His sorrow here is not over corporate units, but over individuals who have rejected their only hope of salvation. Paul's sorrow is not

11. Sanders, *The God Who Risks*, 121. Boyd's view is somewhat different. He understands Paul to be refuting the view that God has broken his covenant promise to the Jews by basing the new covenant on grace alone. Paul responds to this problem, Boyd says, by pointing out that "God's covenant promises have never been based on works" (*God of the Possible*, 143). That is indeed Paul's concern in Rom. 3:21–4:25, and Rom. 9 echoes it, but more is going on in Rom. 9.

based on the fact that Israel has lost its status as God's only corporate people. In itself, that is cause for rejoicing, for it opens the door for Gentiles to enter God's kingdom, and in time there will be a great ingathering of Jews as well (11:11–32). Paul's sorrow is over the present unbelief of individuals, and in Romans 9 he seeks to show why that unbelief exists.

To show this, he explains how God has in the past sovereignly discriminated within the covenant family. He chose Isaac over Ishmael (9:6–9) and Jacob over Esau (vv. 10–13).[12] Isaac and Jacob become patriarchal heads of the covenant family, so there is a corporate aspect to God's election. But they are also individuals, and they illustrate the principle that "not all who are descended from Israel are Israel" (v. 6). An individual's destiny is not determined by his membership in a corporate group, but by God's grace to him as an individual. That is even more clearly evident in the case of Pharaoh (vv. 16–18). Pharaoh is not a potential covenant patriarch. God rejects him simply as an individual.

It is impossible to avoid the conclusion that Paul is making the same point with respect to God's rejection of the unbelieving Israelites. To be sure, Paul's illustrations of election are taken from the sphere of historical election. But Paul is not distinguishing between historical and eternal election. Rather, he is focusing on the principles that these two forms of election have in common: in both cases, election is by grace, apart from works (v. 12). In all these cases, election is by God's purpose (v. 11) and calling (v. 12). Esau is reprobate (whether historically or eternally) before he is born (v. 11), hated by God (v. 13). Certainly the same is true of the

12. It is not necessary to say that Ishmael and Esau are eternally damned. They are historically nonelect, but the passage does not teach that they are eternally nonelect. Paul here uses aspects of historical election to illustrate his view of eternal election.

Jews of Paul's time who reject Jesus:[13] they reject him because God has not called them. They are reprobate by the sovereign decision of God.

Otherwise, the question of verse 14, "What then shall we say? Is God unjust?" makes no sense. The question can arise only because, on Paul's view, the Jews' unbelief is due to God's sovereign decision. If their unbelief were due only to their free decision, no one would say that God is unjust to condemn them. Paul emphasizes the point by quoting Exodus 33:19:

> "I will have mercy on whom I have mercy,
>   and I will have compassion on whom I have
>   compassion." (v. 15, repeated in v. 18)

And he adds, "It does not, therefore, depend on man's desire or effort, but on God's mercy" (v. 16).

The same is true of Pharaoh. Paul quotes Exodus 9:16, where God tells Moses to say to Pharaoh for him, "I raised you up for this very purpose, that I might display my power in you and that my name might be proclaimed in all the earth" (v. 17).

Again a question arises:

> One of you will say to me: "Then why does God still blame us? For who resists his will?" But who are you, O man, to talk back to God? "Shall what is formed say to him who formed it, 'Why did you make me like this?'" Does not the potter have the right to make out of the same lump of clay some pottery for noble purposes and some for common use? (vv. 19–21)

---

13. One cannot assume that all of those Israelites who failed to respond to the preaching of Paul were eternally reprobate. Paul doubtless realized that some might come to Christ at a later time. He is concerned in Rom. 9–11 about the great number of Jews who have rejected the gospel. And his answer is that God has first rejected them some perhaps temporarily, some permanently.

Paul might have said that God is just, because Pharaoh and the others made free decisions to reject God. That would have been true, as far as it goes. But Paul wants to present a deeper answer, because it is also his answer to the question of Israel's unbelief. His answer is that Israel's unbelief comes from God's sovereign decision. In that light, we can also understand the next question:

> What if God, choosing to show his wrath and make his power known, bore with great patience the objects of his wrath—prepared for destruction? (v. 22)

None of this compromises Israel's own responsibility. Paul stresses that, too, in 9:30–10:21. But then again, in 11:1–10, he emphasizes God's sovereignty. The remnant is "chosen by grace" (v. 5). The others are hardened, for God has given them a spirit of stupor (vv. 7–10).

These are hard sayings, and I myself could wish that the passage presented fewer challenges to those who would expound it in today's theological environment. But I cannot escape the conclusion that for Paul the unbelief, as well as the belief, of individual Israelites is due to God's sovereign choice.

How Can God Act "Now" If He Acts "Always"?

Sanders asks, "If God is the cause of everything, then why single out certain things as being 'from God'?"[14] What is special about his special providences, miracles, and mighty redemptive acts? The answer, I think, is that although God brings all things to pass, there are some events in which he (1) does things of special interest to human beings, (2) reveals himself in extraordinary ways, and/or (3) acts in such a way as to vividly contrast his power with that of finite agents. He

14. Sanders, *The God Who Risks*, 83.

also sometimes (4) performs special actions that bear his seal, that unambiguously advance his purposes in history. Thus, Gamaliel in Acts 5:39 says that "if [the preaching of Christ] is from God, you will not be able to stop these men; you will only find yourselves fighting against God."

All things are from God, but too often we fail to acknowledge his universal sovereignty, and he performs extraordinary actions to gain our attention, as well as to accomplish his purposes.[15] Those extraordinary actions are "from God" in a special or narrow sense. But, as Gamaliel well knew, these events underscore God's overall sovereignty, rather than calling it into question.

Other Open-Theist Objections

Other open-theist objections to God's exhaustive foreordination of events are (1) that in Scripture God's will is not irresistible, (2) that exhaustive divine foreordination is incompatible with libertarian human freedom, and (3) that in Scripture God does not know the future exhaustively and therefore cannot have full control over it. I will deal with these objections in subsequent chapters.

---

15. Compare my discussion of miracle in my forthcoming *The Doctrine of God,* chap. 13. The distinction in Scripture between miracle and providence is not sharp. Miracles are relatively extraordinary demonstrations of God's lordship.

SEVEN

Is God's Will Irresistible?

Another objection of open theists to the doctrine of exhaustive divine foreordination is that God does not always get what he wants in the Bible. Creatures sometimes "thwart" God's will. Therefore, God must take risks.

Nicole points out that to open theists, these risks are great indeed. For them, God's frustration is not occasional, but frequent. He took a big risk when he created free angels, and Satan defected with many fallen angels, generating the "enormous problem of evil." God expected Adam and Eve to remain upright, but they did not. In time, evil became rampant, so that God regretted having made mankind and brought about an "almost complete annihilation of humanity." God risked saving Noah and his family, but that didn't work out, either. His gambles turned out so badly that only the death of his own Son could save the situation. But even that turned out to be insufficient, since many people have refused to believe and so have suffered devastating consequences.[1]

1. Roger Nicole, "A Review Article: God of the Possible?" *Reformation and Revival* 10, no. 1 (winter, 2001), 182–83. I have paraphrased and summarized Nicole's description.

Sanders admits that, at a very broad level, God's will is always done. In response to passages like Psalm 135:6 and Daniel 4:35, he says:

> In terms of the boundaries, structures and goals of the project that God has sovereignly established, there is no question whatsoever that God gets what he wants. God can create a world, provide for it and grant it his love without anyone or anything being able to thwart his overarching desires. If God decides to create a world with persons capable of reciprocating the divine love and if God establishes genuine give-and-take relations with them, then it is proper to say that nothing can stymie God's intentions.[2]

At more specific levels, however, Sanders believes that God's will can be thwarted:

> If God does not force the creatures to reciprocate his love, then the possibility is introduced that at least some of them may fail to enter into the divine love, and thus certain of God's specific desires might be thwarted. If God wants a world in which the possibility exists that God might not get everything he wants, then in an ultimate sense the divine will is not thwarted. It is important to note that if in some cases God does not get what he wants, it is ultimately because of the decision *God* made to create the sort of world in which God does not get everything he wants.[3]

In distinguishing different levels of divine wants, desires, and will,[4] Sanders is on traditional ground. Even Calvinistic

---

2. John Sanders, *The God Who Risks* (Downers Grove, Ill.: InterVarsity Press, 1998), 228–29.

3. Ibid., 229.

4. It would be convenient if we could link each of these levels to a technical term—for example, if we could use *will* for the highest level and *desire* for lower levels. However, in Scripture, the terms translated "will," "desire," "want," and "wish" are all used at multiple levels.

---

theologians grant that there are some states of affairs that God genuinely values (and therefore wants or desires), but does not bring about. For example, it is plain that God desires, in some sense, all human beings to worship him, to honor their parents, to refrain from murder, adultery, etc. But that divine desire is unsatisfied.

We can understand such levels of desire from our own experience. We have many different kinds of wants and pleasures, and we arrange them according to our priorities. Some things we want more than others. Some we cannot achieve, and so we settle for others. We postpone fulfilling some desires until others are realized. Sometimes one must be realized before another. Some are not compatible with others, and so we must choose between them. For such reasons, some of our desires are unfulfilled, temporarily or permanently.

Often our prioritizing of desires is due to our weakness, but sometimes not. One may desire an ice-cream cone and have easy access to one, but voluntarily postpone fulfilling that desire until a piece of work is finished. He may value finishing the job more than eating the ice-cream cone, or perhaps not. Maybe he actually values the ice cream more, but believes he will get more enjoyment from it after the job is done. So our decision-making process is often complicated. The interrelationships among our many desires, and among the various means of achieving them, are complex.

Here we see some analogy to the complexities of God's will. God also has many desires, variously valued and prioritized. Some he achieves immediately. But since he has created a world in time and has given to that world a history and a goal, some of his desires, by virtue of his own eternal plan, must await the passage of time. Further, there are some good things that, by virtue of the nature of God's plan, will never be realized. God's plan is consistent with itself, respecting the integrity of creatures. If God has ordained that Joe will have exactly three children, that excludes the possibility that he will have five, even though two more children might (in the abstract) be a good thing. And God's broad intentions for history evidently exclude the blessing of a world existing without any history of evil.

So theologians have made various distinctions within the larger concept of the will of God. God's will is, of course, one. But it is also complex, so some have distinguished different aspects of it as "wills," in the plural. We should be careful with this language, but it does make it easier for us to consider the complications of our topic.

Antecedent and Consequent Wills

Some theologians have distinguished between God's antecedent and consequent wills. God's general valuation of some things as good we may call his *antecedent* will; his specific choices among those good things (in view of the overall nature of the world he intends to make) may be called his *consequent* will. Roman Catholic, Lutheran, and Arminian theologians have used the antecedent-consequent distinction to make room for libertarian freedom. On their view, God's antecedent will includes the salvation of all men. His consequent will, however, awaits the (libertarian) free decisions of human beings. Those who choose to believe, God blesses; those who do not, he condemns to eternal punishment. These blessings and curses come by his consequent will, which itself is a response to human choices.

In my view, these theologians are right in saying that God antecedently wants everyone to be saved. Universal salvation is certainly a desirable state of affairs. They are also right to claim that, in view of the actual historical situation, God does not bring that result to pass. There is no harm in calling this second volition "consequent." In his eternal plan, God does determine not to achieve certain good things. But I reject the notion of libertarian freedom often connected with this distinction. As we have seen, God's choice comes first. Human choices are effects of, and responses to, the divine choice.

Decretive and Preceptive Wills

Reformed theologians have often rejected the antecedent-consequent distinction, because of its association with libertarian freedom. But they have adopted a rather similar distinction, between God's decretive and preceptive wills. God's *decretive* will (or simply his "decree") is synonymous with his foreordination, which we discussed in chapter 5. It is his eternal purpose, by which he foreordains everything that comes to pass. God's *preceptive* will[5] is his valuations, particularly as revealed to us in his Word (his "precepts"). God's decretive will cannot be successfully opposed; what God has decreed will certainly take place. It is possible, however, for creatures to disobey God's preceptive will—and they often do so.

This distinction is somewhat similar to the antecedent-consequent distinction, although the two distinctions tend to appear in different theological traditions. God's preceptive will, like the antecedent will, consists of his valuation of every possible and actual state of affairs. His decretive will, like the consequent will, determines what will actually happen. The difference between decretive and consequent is that the concept of a decretive will excludes libertarianism. God's decision as to what will actually happen is not based on his foreknowledge of the libertarian free choices of men.

5. The term *preceptive* is somewhat misleading, for it does not always have to do with literal precepts (God's laws, commandments). Sometimes God's preceptive will refers to states of affairs that God sees as desirable, but which he chooses not to bring about (e.g., Ezek. 18:23; 2 Peter 3:9). Still, I will use *preceptive* because of customary usage, and because I don't know of any superior term.

But even on a Reformed view, God's sovereign choices do take into account the nature of the world that he has chosen to make. As with Joe's children, God will not bring about an event that is inconsistent with another event that he has ordained. In that way, God respects the integrity of each event, person, and thing in his eternal plan. So each part of his plan excludes from it some otherwise possible states of affairs, some of which may be good in themselves. So God genuinely values many states of affairs that are not compatible with the particular story he has chosen to tell in history. In one sense, then, God's plan is limited by the nature of the creatures included in the plan. But that is only to say that God's plan is limited by its own consistency and integrity.

Although I shall argue later that God's thoughts are ultimately timeless, rather than temporally successive, it is helpful to represent God's thought as if it were in two stages. First, God evaluates every possible state of affairs (antecedent, preceptive). Second, he chooses among these values (decretive, consequent), rejecting some and accepting others for the sake of his historical drama.

Does Scripture warrant this distinction? Here are some passages that use the words *thought, intent, pleasure, purpose, counsel,* and *will* to refer to God's decretive will:

> You intended to harm me, but God intended it for good to accomplish what is now being done, the saving of many lives. (Gen. 50:20)

> At that time Jesus said, "I praise you, Father, Lord of heaven and earth, because you have hidden these things from the wise and learned, and revealed them to little children. Yes, Father, for this was your good pleasure." (Matt. 11:25–26)

This man was handed over to you by God's set purpose and foreknowledge; and you, with the help of wicked men, put him to death by nailing him to the cross. (Acts 2:23)

Therefore God has mercy on whom he wants to have mercy, and he hardens whom he wants to harden.
One of you will say to me: "Then why does God still blame us? For who resists his will?" (Rom. 9:18–19)

In him we were also chosen, having been predestined according to the plan of him who works out everything in conformity with the purpose of his will. (Eph. 1:11)

(Compare Pss. 51:18; 115:3; Isa. 46:10; Jer. 49:20; 50:45; Dan. 4:17; James 1:18; Rev. 4:11.) I would say that God's "paths" (or "ways") in Romans 11:33 should also be taken in the decretive sense, although elsewhere the term is almost always preceptive.

Here are some passages in which these terms are used in a preceptive sense:

Not everyone who says to me, "Lord, Lord," will enter the kingdom of heaven, but only he who does the will of my Father who is in heaven. (Matt. 7:21)

Therefore do not be foolish, but understand what the Lord's will is. (Eph. 5:17; cf. 6:6)[6]

(Compare Pss. 5:4; 103:21; Matt. 12:50; John 4:34; 7:17; Rom. 12:2; 1 Thess. 4:3; 5:18; Heb. 13:21; 1 Peter 4:2.) These passages refer literally to precepts of God.

The following passages refer, not to precepts as such, but to desirable states of affairs that God does not ordain—states

6. "Will" here translates *thelema*, which in 1:11 is clearly decretive.

of affairs that I include within the general category of God's preceptive will:

> Do I take any pleasure in the death of the wicked? declares the Sovereign LORD. Rather, am I not pleased when they turn from their ways and live? (Ezek. 18:23)

> The Lord is not slow in keeping his promise, as some understand slowness. He is patient with you, not wanting anyone to perish, but everyone to come to repentance. (2 Peter 3:9)

There are other passages in which God expresses a desire for repentance from human beings, which may or may not be forthcoming (Isa. 30:18; 65:2; Lam. 3:31–36; Ezek. 33:11; Hos. 11:7–8).

Sanders's Distinction

Sanders's view is like the traditional distinction between antecedent and consequent, in which God's will is limited by human free choice. But Sanders goes further than that. We will recall from chapter 6 that Sanders denies that all weather comes from God. So evidently for Sanders human libertarian freedom is not the only limit on God's control of the world. He also believes that the natural world itself has a kind of autonomy, so that events in nature, as well as human free choices, sometimes take God by surprise.

Sanders is right to say that in one sense God's will cannot be thwarted, and that in another sense it can be. I also agree with him that the thwarting of God's will takes place in more or less specific matters, rather than in the broad outlines of his plan. I also agree with him that God allows his will to be thwarted because of the nature of the creatures he has made, because of their integrity and the integrity of his plan.

But integrity is one thing, and autonomy is something else. If, as I indicated in chapter 5, God brings about everything that happens, then there is no room for autonomy, either in nature or in human beings. God has planned and foreordained everything that happens, so nothing takes him by surprise.

I shall indicate in the next chapter why I believe that libertarian freedom is unscriptural. As for the autonomy of the natural world, Scripture never hints at any such thing. As I indicated in chapters 5 and 6, the worldview of the biblical writers is deeply personalistic. For them, the events of nature are the works of God.

Sanders and other open theists evidently think that since God's will is sometimes thwarted, according to Scripture, the natural world must be to some degree autonomous and human beings must be free in a libertarian sense. But that conclusion does not follow at all. There is a perfectly adequate explanation as to why God's will is not always fulfilled, which has nothing to do with theories of autonomy or libertarianism. That explanation is simply this: God's will is sometimes thwarted because he wills it to be, because he has given one of his desires precedence over another.

The Efficacy of God's Will

But the important question with regard to open theism is not whether God's will is always done, in every sense of divine willing. Rather, the question is whether God can fail in anything he intends to do. In other words, can creatures ever thwart God's decretive will? On this question, Scripture is entirely clear and unambiguous. Simply put, God's power always accomplishes his purpose. God does not intend to bring about everything he values, but he never fails to bring about what he intends. Creatures may oppose him, to be sure, but they cannot prevail.

Now we should remember that God decrees, not only the end of history, but also the events of every moment of time. For his own reasons, he has chosen to delay the fulfillment of his intentions for the end of history, and to bring about those intentions through a complicated historical sequence of events. In that sequence, his purposes appear sometimes to suffer defeat, sometimes to achieve victory. But each apparent defeat actually makes his eventual victory all the more glorious. The cross of Jesus is, of course, the chief example of this principle. So God intends, not only his ultimate triumph, but also his apparent defeats in history. He intends that history be exactly as it is. Therefore, all his decrees, both those for history and for the consummation of history, always come to pass.

So, over and over, Scripture affirms that God's purposes will prevail. And they do prevail, not only at the end of history, and not only in their broad outlines, but throughout history, in all specific situations. Indeed, if my account in chapter 5 is correct, they prevail in everything that happens. Nothing is too hard for God (Jer. 32:27); nothing seems marvelous to him (Zech. 8:6); with him nothing is impossible (Gen. 18:14; Matt. 19:26; Luke 1:37). So his purposes will always prevail. Against Assyria, he says:

> "Surely, as I have planned, so it will be,
>   and as I have purposed, so it will stand.
> I will crush the Assyrian. . . ."
> This is the plan determined for the whole world;
>   this is the hand stretched out over all nations.
> For the LORD Almighty has purposed, and who can
>   thwart him?
>   His hand is stretched out, and who can turn it back?
>   (Isa. 14:24–27; cf. Job 42:2; Jer. 23:20)

When God expresses his eternal purposes in words, through his prophets, those prophecies will surely come to pass (Deut.

18:21–22; Isa. 31:2).[7] God sometimes represents his word as his active agent that inevitably accomplishes his bidding:

> [As the rain waters the earth,] so is my word that goes
>   out from my mouth:
>   It will not return to me empty,
> but will accomplish what I desire
>   and achieve the purpose for which I sent it. (Isa.
>   55:11; cf. Zech. 1:6)

So the wise teacher reminds us,

> There is no wisdom, no insight, no plan
>   that can succeed against the LORD. (Prov. 21:30; cf.
>   16:9; 19:21)

Scripture speaks often of God's purpose in terms of "what pleases him" or "his good pleasure." God's pleasure will surely be realized:

> I say: My purpose will stand,
>   and I will do all that I please. (Isa. 46:10)

> All the peoples of the earth
>   are regarded as nothing.
> He does as he pleases
>   with the powers of heaven
>   and the peoples of the earth.
> No one can hold back his hand
>   or say to him, "What have you done?" (Dan. 4:35)

---

7. Not every prophecy in Scripture is an expression of God's eternal purpose. Some prophecies indicate what God will do in various possible situations. Sometimes, therefore, he announces judgment, but "relents" when people repent (see Jer. 18:5–10). I shall discuss this issue again in connection with God's unchangeability. See also Richard Pratt, "Prophecy and Historical Contingency," at www.thirdmill.org.

At that time Jesus said, "I praise you, Father, Lord of heaven and earth, because you have hidden these things from the wise and learned, and revealed them to little children. Yes, Father, for this was your good pleasure. (Matt. 11:25–26)

In love he predestined us to be adopted as his sons through Jesus Christ, in accordance with his pleasure and will. (Eph. 1:4–5; cf. v. 9)

To illustrate the efficacy of God's purposes in our lives, Scripture uses the image of the potter and the clay (Isa. 29:16; 45:9; 64:8; Jer. 18:1–10; Rom. 9:19–24). As easily as the potter molds his clay, making one vessel for one purpose and another vessel for another purpose, so God deals with people. His purpose will prevail, and the clay has no right to complain to the potter about it. Sanders agrees that in these passages the clay has no right to complain against the potter. But he believes that the potter rejects some pieces of clay, not because of his own sovereign purpose, but because "this particular clay has rejected the divine project." So, he says, "the potter-clay metaphor must be understood in terms of the give-and-take relationship that God has sovereignly established. It should not be understood as teaching divine control of all things."[8] However, the potter's total control over the clay is implicit in the metaphor itself and explicit in Romans 9:19–21, where it is the potter's initiative to "make out of the same lump of clay some pottery for noble purposes and some for common use." In Romans 9, it is plain, both on the level of the metaphor and on the level of history (the relationship between Jews and Christians), that God himself is the ultimate source of distinction.

8. Sanders, *The God Who Risks*, 87.

The general efficacy of God's purpose forms the background for the Reformed doctrine of irresistible grace. As we mentioned earlier, sinners do resist God's purposes; indeed, that is a significant theme in Scripture (Isa. 65:12; Matt. 23:37–39; Luke 7:30; Acts 7:51; Eph. 4:30; 1 Thess. 5:19; Heb. 4:2; 12:25). But the point of the doctrine is that their resistance does not succeed against the Lord. When God intends to bring someone to faith in Christ, he cannot fail, although for his own reasons he may choose to wrestle with a person for a long time before achieving that purpose.[9]

So Scripture regularly teaches that when God elects, calls, and regenerates someone in Christ, through the Spirit, that work accomplishes his saving purpose. When God gives his people a new heart, it is certain that "they will follow my decrees and be careful to keep my laws" (Ezek. 11:20; cf. 36:26–27). When God gives new life (John 5:21), we cannot send it back to him. Jesus said, "All that the Father gives me will come to me" (John 6:37). If God foreknows (i.e., befriends) someone, he will certainly predestine him to be conformed to the likeness of Christ, to be called, to be justified, and to be glorified in heaven (Rom. 8:29–30). "God has mercy on whom he wants to have mercy, and he hardens whom he wants to harden" (Rom. 9:18, referring to Ex. 33:19). The psalmist says:

> Blessed are those you choose
>> and bring near to live in your courts!
> We are filled with the good things of your house,
>> of your holy temple. (Ps. 65:4)

---

9. There are also situations where people who appear to be elect turn away from God and prove themselves not to be among his people. There are also cases where God chooses someone for a task and for a limited kind of fellowship with him, without the intention of giving him the full benefits of salvation. Judas is one example (John 6:70), as is national Israel, which, because of unbelief, lost its special status as God's elect nation.

Paul adds, "For God did not appoint us to suffer wrath but to receive salvation through our Lord Jesus Christ" (1 Thess. 5:9).

Like his word, therefore, God's grace will never return to him void.

We can summarize the biblical teaching about the efficacy of God's rule in the following passages, which speak for themselves:

> But the plans of the LORD stand firm forever,
>> the purposes of his heart through all generations.
>>> (Ps. 33:11)

> Our God is in heaven;
>> he does whatever pleases him. (Ps. 115:3)

> The LORD does whatever pleases him,
>> in the heavens and on the earth,
>> in the seas and all their depths. (Ps. 135:6)

> "You are my witnesses," declares the Lord, "that I am
>> God.
>> Yes, and from ancient days I am he.
> No one can deliver out of my hand.
>> When I act, who can reverse it?" (Isa. 43:12–13; cf.
>> Deut. 32:39)

> These are the words of him who is holy and true, who holds the key of David. What he opens no one can shut, and what he shuts, no one can open. (Rev. 3:7)

Do We Have Genuine Freedom?

We come now to perhaps the central issue in the debate concerning open theism. In my judgment, the concept of human freedom in the libertarian sense is the engine that drives open theism, often called freewill theism. For the open theist, libertarian free will serves as a kind of grid, through which all other theological assertions must pass—a general criterion for testing the truth of all other doctrines. For the open theist, only those doctrines that are compatible with libertarian freedom are worthy of consideration; all others must be rejected at the outset. And typically, open theists do not argue the case (such as there is) for libertarian freedom; rather, they assume it.[1] It is their presupposition.

---

1. I may have missed something, of course, but in the major writings of the open theists, I have yet to find a serious argument for libertarian freedom. These authors express much distaste for views like Calvinism that deny such freedom, and they speak glowingly of the freshness, spontaneity, creativity, newness, etc., that libertarianism brings us. They also mention some Scripture passages, but there is always a great leap from the text to the libertarian conclusion. They also suggest, as we shall see, that libertarianism is necessary for moral responsibility, but they present the argument for that proposition sketchily, and they ignore the objections commonly raised against it. There are respectable (though, to me, not persuasive) arguments for libertarianism in the secular philosophical literature, but not in the literature of open theism.

When open theists speak of "genuine," "significant," "real," or "authentic" freedom, they have libertarian freedom in mind. Open theist William Hasker defines libertarian freedom as follows:

> An agent is free with respect to a given action at a given time if at that time it is within the agent's power to perform the action and also in the agent's power to refrain from the action.[2]

R. K. McGregor Wright, a critic of open theism, defines this view as

> the belief that the human will has an inherent power to choose with equal ease between alternatives. This is commonly called "the power of contrary choice" or "the liberty of indifference." This belief does not claim that there are no influences that might affect the will, but it does insist that normally the will can overcome these factors and choose in spite of them. Ultimately, the will is free from any necessary causation. In other words, it is autonomous from outside determination.[3]

Libertarians emphasize that our choices are not determined in advance by God. On their view, God may be the first cause of the universe in general, but in the sphere of human decisions, we are the first causes of our actions. We have a godlike independence when we make free choices.

Furthermore, as Wright's definition implies, in libertarianism our decisions must also be independent of ourselves in a certain sense, paradoxical as that may sound. On the libertarian view, our character may influence our decisions, as may our immediate desires. But we always have the freedom to

---

2. William Hasker, "A Philosophical Perspective," in OG, 136–37.
3. R. K. McGregor Wright, *No Place for Sovereignty* (Downers Grove, Ill.: InterVarsity Press, 1996), 43–44.

No Other God

choose contrary to our character and our desires, however strong.

This position assumes that there is a part of human nature that we might call the will, which is independent of every other aspect of our being, and which can, therefore, make a decision contrary to every motivation.

Libertarians maintain that only if we have this kind of radical freedom can we be held responsible for our actions. Their principle is simple enough: if our decisions are caused by anything or anyone (including our own desires), they are not properly our decisions, and we cannot be held responsible for them. To be responsible, we must be able to do otherwise. And if our actions are caused by anything other than our free will, we are not able to do otherwise, and we are therefore not responsible.

Some open theists seem to believe that all our decisions are free in this sense. Rice, for example, admits that God controls many things that happen in nature, but he insists that "where human decision is presupposed . . . God cannot achieve his objectives unilaterally. He requires our cooperation."[4] The word "cannot" seems to imply that God can never determine or foreordain a human choice.

Boyd, however, seems to think differently. He grants that God sometimes hardens a person's heart and thereby determines the person's choice to sin. For example, although Boyd seeks to mitigate the implications of the fact that Jesus predicted Judas's betrayal (John 6:64, 70–71; 13:18–19; 17:12), he concedes the heart of the matter:

> Scripture elsewhere teaches that a dreadful time may come when God discerns that it is useless to strive with a particular individual or a group of people any longer. At this point, he withdraws his Spirit from these people, hardens

4. Richard Rice, "Biblical Support for a New Perspective," in OG, 56.

---

their hearts, and thus seals their destinies (e.g. Gen. 6:3; Rom. 1:24–27).[5]

On Boyd's account, Judas's decision to betray Jesus was not free in the libertarian sense. Judas was not then equally able to choose either alternative.[6] He mentions also Josiah, Cyrus, and the parents of John the Baptist as examples of God restricting "the scope of freedom these individuals could exercise *as it pertained to particular foreordained activities*."[7] Boyd implies that many human decisions are not free in this sense. Pinnock, too, seems to grant that although God generally influences us "persuasively," rather than "coercively," there are exceptions. He says that "to reduce God's power to persuasion would make God too passive—it would be an overreaction against almightiness."[8]

A Critique of Libertarianism

Libertarianism has a long history in Christian theology. Most of the church fathers held more or less this position until Augustine, during the Pelagian controversy, called it into question.[9] Since then, there has been a contest between the Augustinian and the Pelagian conceptions of freedom, resulting sometimes in various unstable mixtures of the two. Both Luther[10] and Calvin[11] followed Augustine, but Molinists,

5. Gregory A. Boyd, *God of the Possible* (Grand Rapids: Baker, 2000), 38.

6. But Judas was certainly morally responsible for what he did. Scripture calls him wicked, and he deserves God's judgment. This fact calls into question the open-theist view that libertarian freedom is the ground of moral responsibility.

7. Boyd, *God of the Possible*, 34 (emphasis his).

8. Clark H. Pinnock, "Systematic Theology," in OG, 116. Compare his "Between Classical and Process Theism," in *Process Theology*, ed. Ronald H. Nash (Grand Rapids: Baker, 1987), 309–27.

9. Those Calvinists who place great weight on antiquity and tradition will have to concede, therefore, that the oldest extracanonical traditions do not favor their position.

10. Martin Luther, *The Bondage of the Will* (London: J. Clarke, 1957).

11. See many writings of John Calvin, especially *Concerning the Eternal Predestination of God* (London: James Clarke, 1961). The classic Calvinist refu-

Socinians, and Arminians offered vigorous defenses of libertarianism. Today the libertarian view prevails in much of evangelical Christianity and among Christian philosophers.[12] Theologically, it is defended by traditional Arminians,[13] open theists, process thinkers,[14] and many others. Few theologians oppose it today, except for self-conscious Calvinists, and even some thinkers in the Reformed tradition gravitate toward libertarianism[15] or speak unclearly on the subject.[16]

But libertarianism is subject to severe criticisms:

1. The biblical data cited in chapter 5 about God's sovereign control over human decisions, even human sins, are in-

---

tation of libertarianism is Jonathan Edwards, *Freedom of the Will* (New Haven: Yale University Press, 1973).

12. Many Christian philosophers believe that libertarian freedom is essential to an adequate answer to the problem of evil. Alvin Plantinga's argument has been especially influential in this connection. See his *God, Freedom, and Evil* (Grand Rapids: Eerdmans, 1974).

13. The most cogent and complete Arminian argument, in my view, is Jack Cottrell's *What the Bible Says About God the Ruler* (Joplin, Mo.: College Press, 1984). See also the other two books in his trilogy on the doctrine of God.

14. For example, John B. Cobb, Jr., and David Ray Griffin, *Process Theology: An Introductory Exposition* (Philadelphia: Westminster Press, 1976).

15. See, e.g., Plantinga's influential argument in *God, Freedom, and Evil*.

16. See, e.g., Benjamin W. Farley, *The Providence of God in Reformed Perspective* (Grand Rapids: Baker, 1988), and my review in *Westminster Theological Journal* 51 (1989): 397–400. Richard Muller, in his "Grace, Election, and Contingent Choice: Arminius's Gambit and the Reformed Response," in *The Grace of God: The Bondage of the Will*, ed. Thomas R. Schreiner and Bruce A. Ware (Grand Rapids: Baker, 1995), 2:270, says: "It was never the Reformed view that the moral acts of human beings are predetermined, any more than it was ever the Reformed view that the fall of Adam was willed by God to the exclusion of Adam's free choice to sin." I agree that Reformed theology recognizes Adam's choice as free, but only in a compatibilist sense, which I shall describe later. Contrary to Muller, Reformed theologians did teach that God ordained the Fall (otherwise, where did the debate between supralapsarians and infralapsarians as to the place of the Fall among God's decrees originate?) and therefore ordained at least one human moral decision. And Scripture mentions many more human moral decisions ordained by God, as we saw in chapter 5. In fairness to Muller, he does recommend a compatibilist formulation on p. 269. But compatibilist freedom does not exclude divine predetermination of moral acts, as he suggests it does.

---

compatible with libertarianism. Scripture makes clear that our choices are part of God's eternal plan, even though we are fully responsible for them.

2. Scripture does not explicitly teach the existence of libertarian freedom. There is no passage that can be construed to mean that the human will is independent of God's plan and of the rest of the human personality. Libertarians generally don't even try to establish their position by direct exegesis. Rather, they attempt to deduce it from other biblical concepts, such as human responsibility itself and the divine commands, exhortations, and pleadings[17] that indicate human responsibility. But in this attempt, they accept a rather large burden of proof, which their arguments do not bear. Libertarianism is a rather technical philosophical notion, which makes various assumptions about causality, the relationship of will to action, the relationship of will to character and desire, and the limitation of God's sovereignty. It is a huge order to try to derive all these technical concepts from the biblical view of human responsibility, and I shall try to show below that libertarians' attempts to do so have been far from successful. And if they fail to bear this burden of proof, then we must abandon either libertarianism or *sola Scriptura*.

3. Scripture never grounds human responsibility in libertarian freedom, or, for that matter, in any other kind of freedom. We are responsible because God has made us, owns us, and has a right to evaluate our conduct. Therefore, according to Scripture, God's authority is the necessary and sufficient ground of human responsibility.

Now sometimes our ability or inability is relevant to moral guilt. In Exodus 21:12–14 and Numbers 35:10–34, Scripture distinguishes between murder and manslaughter. The punishment for manslaughter is less, presumably because it is less

17. In my view, God's commands and pleas to human beings are expressions of his preceptive will, as I discussed in chapter 7.

No Other God

avoidable. (Ex. 21:13 makes the point theistically: "God lets it happen.") And those who are ignorant of the Lord's will are beaten with fewer blows, presumably because ignorance is a kind of inability (Luke 12:47–48). But even in this case there is punishment. And not every kind of inability limits moral or legal liability. Scripture never suggests that divine foreordination of a human decision makes the human agent less responsible—quite the contrary. Judas is a clear example, as we saw earlier. Scripture never suggests that libertarian freedom, or lack of it, has any relevance at all to moral responsibility.

4. Nor does Scripture indicate that God places any positive value on libertarian freedom (even granting that it exists). This is a significant point, because the freewill defense against the problem of evil argues that God places such a high value on human free choice that he gave it to creatures even at the risk that they might bring evil into the world. One would imagine, then, that Scripture would abound with statements to the effect that causeless free actions by creatures are terribly important to God, that they bring him glory and are essential to human personhood and dignity. But Scripture never suggests that God honors causeless choice in any way or even recognizes its existence.

5. Indeed, on the contrary, Scripture teaches that in heaven, the consummate state of human existence, we will not be free to sin. So the highest state of human existence will be a state without libertarian freedom.

6. Scripture never judges anyone's conduct by reference to his libertarian freedom. Scripture never declares someone innocent because his conduct was not free in the libertarian sense; not does it ever declare someone guilty by pointing to his libertarian freedom. Judas's betrayal of Jesus, as we have seen, was not a free act in the libertarian sense, even on Boyd's analysis. Yet he was certainly responsible. It was a wicked act and deserved God's judgment. Scripture never refers to freedom in a demonstrably libertarian sense.

7. In civil courts, libertarian freedom is never assumed to be a condition of moral responsibility. Consider Hubert, the bank robber. If guilt presupposed libertarian freedom, then in order to show that Hubert is guilty, the prosecutor would have to show that his decision to rob a bank had no cause. But what evidence could a prosecutor bring forth to show that? Proving a negative is always difficult, and it would clearly be impossible to show that Hubert's inner decision was completely independent of any divine decree, natural cause, character, or motive. The same thing would be true for any criminal prosecution. Libertarianism would make it impossible to prove the guilt of anybody at all.

8. Indeed, civil courts normally assume the opposite of libertarianism, namely, that the conduct of criminals arises from motives. Accordingly, courts often spend much time discussing whether the defendant had an adequate motive to commit the crime. If Hubert's action could be shown (contrary to the second point above) to be causeless, independent of motives, then he would likely be judged insane and therefore *not* responsible, rather than guilty. Such an act would be an accident, not a purposeful choice. Indeed, if Hubert's action was completely independent of his character, desires, and motives, one could well ask in what sense this action was really Hubert's.[18] And if it was not Hubert's action, how can he be held responsible for it? We see, then, that rather than being the foundation of moral responsibility, libertarianism destroys it.[19]

18. One libertarian reply is that the will is Hubert's, and so the action is his. But what is meant by "will" here? Does Hubert's will have a character? Does it have preferences or desires? If so, then we are back to actions controlled by one's nature, which libertarianism rejects. Does it have no character at all? Then how is it any different from a mere force that acts at random and is quite separate from anything in Hubert? On that supposition, how can it be Hubert's will?

19. Calvinists and other antilibertarians often make this point in colorful ways. James H. Thornwell says, "As well might a weather-cock be held responsible for its lawless motions as a being whose arbitrary, uncontrollable will is his only law" (*Collected Writings of James Henley Thornwell* [Edinburgh: Banner of

No OTHER GOD

9. Scripture contradicts the proposition that only un-caused decisions are morally responsible. As we saw in chapter 5, God in Scripture often brings about the free actions, and even the sinful actions, of human beings, without in the least diminishing their responsibility. Often, indeed, Scripture speaks of divine foreordination and human responsibility in connection with the same actions in the same contexts. (See Gen. 50:20; 1 Kings 8:58–61; Prov. 16:4–5; Isa. 10:5–15; Jer. 29:10–14; Luke 22:22; John 1:12–13; 6:37; Acts 2:23; 4:27–28; 13:48–14:1; Rom. 9–10; Phil. 2:12–13; Col. 3:1–3.)

10. Scripture denies that we have the independence demanded by libertarian theory. We are not independent of God, for he controls human free actions. Nor can we choose to act independently of our own character and desire. According to Matthew 7:15–20 and Luke 6:43–45, the good tree brings forth good fruit, and the evil tree brings forth evil fruit. If one's heart is right, his actions will be right; otherwise, they will be wrong.

11. Libertarianism, therefore, violates the biblical teaching concerning the unity of human personality in the heart. Scripture teaches that human hearts, and therefore our decisions, are wicked because of the Fall, but that the work of Christ and the regenerating power of the Spirit cleanse the heart so that our actions can be good. We are fallen and renewed as whole persons. This integrity of human personality is not possible in a libertarian construction, for on that view the will must always be independent of the heart and all of our other faculties.

Truth, 1974], 2:180). R. E. Hobart, arguing a secular form of determinism, says, "In proportion as [a person's action] is undetermined, it is just as if his legs should suddenly spring up and carry him off where he did not prefer to go," in "Free Will as Involving Determinism and Inconceivable Without It," *Mind* 43 (1934): 7.

12. If libertarian freedom were necessary for moral responsibility, then God would not be morally responsible for his actions, since he does not have the freedom to act against his holy character. Similarly, the glorified saints in heaven would not be morally responsible, since they cannot fall again into sin. If they did have libertarian freedom, then they could fall into sin, as Origen speculated, in which case the redemption accomplished by Jesus would be insufficient to deal with sin, for it could not reach the inherent waywardness of human free will.

13. Libertarianism is essentially a highly abstract generalization of the principle that inability limits responsibility. Libertarians say that if our decisions are afflicted by any kind of inability, then they are not truly free and we are not truly responsible for them. We saw earlier that there is some truth in this principle, but that it is not always valid, that we are always afflicted by some kinds of inability, and therefore that the principle must be used with great caution. Libertarianism throws caution to the wind.

14. Libertarianism is inconsistent, not only with God's foreordination of all things, but also with his knowledge of future events. If God knew in 1930 that I would wear a green shirt on July 21, 1998,[20] then I am not free to avoid wearing such a shirt on that date. Now libertarians make the point that God can know future events without causing them. But if in 1930 God knew the events of 1998, on what basis did he know them? The Calvinist answer is that he knew them because he knew his own plan for the future. But how, on an Arminian basis, could God have known my free act sixty-eight years in advance? Are my decisions governed by a deterministic chain of finite causes and effects? Is there some force or person other

20. This is, of course, a manner of speaking. I shall argue later that God's knowledge is timeless in a sense. But if God knows timelessly that I will wear a green shirt on July 21, 1998, then in every year, including 1930, he knew I would wear a green shirt on that day.

than God that renders future events certain—a being whom God passively observes? (That is a scary possibility, hardly consistent with monotheism.) None of these answers, nor any other that I can think of, is consistent with libertarianism. For this reason, the open theists, like the Socinian opponents of Calvin, have denied a key element in traditional Arminianism, namely, God's exhaustive foreknowledge. That is a drastic step to take, as we shall see in our later discussion of God's knowledge. It seems to me that they would have been wiser to reject libertarianism, rather than drastically reconstruct their theology to make it consistent with libertarianism.

15. Libertarians like Pinnock and Rice tend to make their view of free will a nonnegotiable, central truth, with which all other theological statements must be made consistent. Libertarian freedom thus takes on a kind of paradigmatic or presuppositional status. But as we have seen, libertarianism is unscriptural. It would be bad enough merely to assert libertarianism contrary to the Bible. But making it a central truth or governing perspective is very dangerous indeed. An incidental error can be corrected without much trouble. But when such an error becomes a major principle, a grid through which all other doctrinal statements are filtered, then a theological system is in grave danger of shipwreck.

16. Philosophical defenses of libertarianism often appeal to intuition as the basis for believing in free will.[21] That is, whenever we are faced with a choice, we feel that we could choose either way, even against our strongest desire.[22] We are

21. See, for example, C. A. Campbell, "The Psychology of Effort of Will," *Proceedings of the Aristotelian Society* 40 (1939–40): 49–74.

22. There is much argument in the literature over whether we can ever choose against our "strongest desire." It seems to me that there is some confusion here as to the different ways in which a desire can be "strong." If the strength in view is an emotional power, then it is plausible that however strong the desire is, we can always choose against it. But if this strength is motivational effectiveness, then of course the strongest desire is that which actually motivates, and it is nonsense to talk about choosing contrary to one's strongest desire.

sometimes conscious, they say, of combating our strongest desires. But whatever one may say in general about an appeal to intuition, it can never be the basis for a universal negative. That is to say, intuition cannot reveal to anyone that his decisions have no cause. We never have anything that might be called a feeling of lack of causation.

Nor can intuition reveal to us that all of our actions do have an outside cause. If all of our actions were determined by an agency outside ourselves, we could not identify that causation by any intuition or feeling, for we would have no way of comparing a feeling of causation with a feeling of noncausation. We can identify influences that sometimes prevail over us and sometimes do not—forces that we sometimes, but not always, resist successfully. But we cannot identify forces that constantly and irresistibly determine our thoughts and behavior. So intuition never reveals to us whether or not we are determined by causes outside ourselves.[23]

17. If libertarianism is true, then God has somehow limited his sovereignty so that he does not bring all things to pass. But Scripture contains no hint that God has limited his sovereignty in any degree. God is the Lord, from Genesis 1 to Revelation 22. He is always completely sovereign. He does whatever pleases him (Ps. 115:3). He works everything out according to the counsel of his will (Eph. 1:11). Furthermore, God's very nature is to be sovereign. Sovereignty is his name, the very meaning of the name Yahweh, in terms of both control and authority.[24] If God limited his sovereignty, he would become something less than Lord of all, something less than God. And if God became something less than God, he would

23. Thanks to Steve Hays for this observation. He also points out that the libertarian appeal to intuition ignores the role of the subconscious in motivating our thoughts and behavior.

24. See my discussion of the meaning of *Yahweh* in *The Doctrine of God* (Phillipsburg, N.J.: P&R Publishing, forthcoming), chaps. 1–7.

No Other God

destroy himself. He would no longer exist. We can see that the consequences of libertarianism are serious indeed.

Other Kinds of Freedom

If we are not free in the libertarian sense, is there any other sense in which we are free? Usually when Scripture uses terms like "free" or "freedom," it refers to spiritual or moral freedom—the freedom to do what is good in God's sight. Scripture teaches that Adam's fall took away our moral freedom, so that apart from grace we cannot please God. Christ sets us free from this bondage:

> Jesus replied, "I tell you the truth, everyone who sins is a slave to sin. Now a slave has no permanent place in the family, but a son belongs to it forever. So if the Son sets you free, you will be free indeed." (John 8:34–36; cf. Rom. 6:15–23; 2 Cor. 3:17)

This is the most important kind of freedom mentioned in Scripture—the freedom from sin, given to us by the redemptive work of Christ. However, it is not a condition of moral responsibility. Those who are bound in slavery to sin are morally responsible, no more or less so than those who are free in Christ.

Scripture also refers to what has been called *compatibilist* freedom: freedom to do what you want to do. Jesus says:

> The good man brings good things out of the good stored up in his heart, and the evil man brings evil things out of the evil stored up in his heart. For out of the overflow of his heart his mouth speaks. (Luke 6:45; cf. Matt. 7:15–20; 12:33–35)

We act and speak, then, according to our character. We follow the deepest desires of our heart. To my knowledge, Scripture never refers to this moral consistency as a kind of freedom, but the concept of heart-act consistency is important in Scripture, and theologians and philosophers have often referred to it as freedom. In everyday life, we regularly think of freedom as doing what we want to do. When we don't do what we want to do, we are either acting irrationally or being forced to act against our will by someone or something outside ourselves.

This kind of freedom is sometimes called compatibilism, because it is compatible with determinism. Determinism is the view that every event (including human actions) has a sufficient cause other than itself. Compatibilist freedom means that even if every act we perform is caused by something outside ourselves (such as natural causes or God), we are still free, for we can still act according to our character and desires.

Pinnock says of compatibilist freedom:

> This is sleight of hand and does not work. Just the fact of our rebellion as sinners against God's will testifies that it is not so. The fall into sin was against the will of God and proves by itself that God does not exercise total control over all events in the world.[25]

Here it is Pinnock who engages in sleight of hand, for he makes some important biblical distinctions disappear. Those are the distinctions I outlined in chapter 7 between God's antecedent and consequent, or preceptive and decretive, wills. Our rebellion is contrary to God's precepts, not contrary to his decrees. And the fact that we can violate his precepts does not imply at all that God lacks total control of the world. Open theists regularly ignore these distinctions, although they are clearly aware of them and grant them from time to time.[26] The plausibility of their argument rests largely on this kind of confusion.

25. Pinnock, "Systematic Theology," 114–15.
26. Recall our discussion of Sanders's view in the preceding chapter. And in Clark H. Pinnock, ed., *The Grace of God and the Will of Man* (Grand Rapids:

NO OTHER GOD

Compatibilist freedom, unlike libertarian freedom, provides a genuine condition for moral responsibility. I noted earlier that in the Mosaic law there are different penalties for murder and manslaughter. The difference is a difference of intention. In manslaughter, the perpetrator does not desire to take life. He does take it, but that action does not reflect his desire. Or, to put it as we usually do, he did not have a motive for murder. That is to say, he did not make a free choice, in the compatibilist sense, to kill.

Still another kind of freedom discussed in this connection is that mentioned in the Westminster Confession of Faith, 9.1:

> God hath endued the will of man with that natural liberty, that it is neither forced, nor, by any absolute necessity of nature, determined to good or evil.

The confession cites as proof texts Matthew 17:12, James 1:14, and Deuteronomy 30:19, which teach that human beings do choose to do what they will, statements compatible with either libertarianism or compatibilism. The confession denies libertarianism in 5.1 and 5.4. But the confession's reference to "absolute necessity of nature" suggests something more than compatibilism: the independence of human choices from sequences of cause and effect within nature, a freedom from natural causation.

As we have seen, Scripture (and the confession at 5.1 and 5.4) affirms that God governs all human actions. At 9.1, the confession suggests that at least some human actions may have no finite cause, though of course its earlier statements

---

Zondervan, 1989), 56, I. Howard Marshall, a defender of libertarianism, says, "We must certainly distinguish between what God would like to happen and what he actually does will to happen, and both of these things can be spoken of as God's will."

imply that those actions have a divine cause. I don't know anything in Scripture that would prove the suggestion of 9.1, but I know of nothing either that would rule it out. Perhaps the value of the confession's statement in 9.1 is to caution us against assuming that our decisions are not only governed by God, but also locked into a chain of finite causes. It opens up the possibility that some events may be determined by God's will, but not determined by anything in creation.

I don't think that the confession's concept of natural liberty has much to do with moral responsibility. But it could be used to refute certain kinds of excuses for wrong actions. For example, if somebody says that he couldn't help stealing, since he was raised in a poor neighborhood, one could reply that there is no reason to think that being raised in a poor neighborhood *necessitates* theft. The thief is not "forced, nor by any absolute necessity of nature, determined to good or evil."

The Problem of Evil

Perhaps the most persuasive argument for libertarianism is that it provides a solution to the problem of evil. The problem of evil is probably the most difficult problem in all of theology, and for many non-Christians it is the Achilles' heel of the theistic worldview.[27] In a nutshell, the problem is this: How could there be any evil in the world, if God exists? If God is good, he does not want evil to exist; if he is all-powerful, he is able to prevent its existence. Nevertheless, evil exists. So, some conclude, either God is not good, or he is not all-powerful, or he does not exist at all.

27. I have discussed the problem of evil more extensively in *Apologetics to the Glory of God* (Phillipsburg, N.J.: P&R Publishing, 1994), 149–90; *Cornelius Van Til* (Phillipsburg, N.J.: P&R Publishing, 1995), 83–86; *The Doctrine of God* (forthcoming), chap. 9. I will not here be discussing, for example, the privation theory of evil or the "soul-making" theodicy, for I do not think that these are of much help, and I have discussed them elsewhere.

The libertarian solution is that God did not bring evil into the world. Rather, he made creatures who are free in the libertarian sense, and they, through their free choices, bring evil into the world. When God granted them this freedom, he took a risk that the world would be infected by evil. But he is not to blame for the result of his risky decision. Pinnock insists:

> Evils happen that are not supposed to happen, that grieve and anger God. Freewill theism is the best way to account for this fact. To say that God hates sin while secretly willing it, to say that God warns us not to fall away though it is impossible, to say that God loves the world while excluding most people from an opportunity of salvation, to say that God warmly invites sinners to come knowing all the while that they cannot possibly do so—such things do not deserve to be called mysteries when that is just a euphemism for nonsense.[28]

In reply, I would reiterate all the arguments previously made in this chapter against the existence of libertarian freedom and its relevance to moral responsibility. If libertarian freedom does not exist, then of course it cannot serve as a solution to the problem of evil.

But even if libertarian freedom did exist, it would not be an adequate solution to the problem. Traditional Arminians, although they don't believe that God causes evil, do believe that he is able to prevent it and that he made the world knowing in advance that evil would enter it. But if God created the world, knowing that sin and evil would certainly enter it, how is his action different from causing or foreordaining evil? It was he who set the process in motion, knowing where it would go. All the things and persons in the world are his creations. The order of events begins in him. If he sets everything in motion, knowing what will happen, how is that different

28. Pinnock, "Systematic Theology," 115.

---

from intending the result? And if the result is evil, how can he avoid the charge that he intended evil?

Open theists hold the same position as Arminians, except that they deny God's foreknowledge of the result. For them, creation was a risky venture. God made the world and gave libertarian freedom to creatures, not knowing what they would do with their freedom. But doesn't this make God into a kind of mad scientist, who "throws together a potentially dangerous combination of chemicals, not knowing if it will result in a hazardous and uncontrollable reaction?"[29] Doesn't this view make God guilty of reckless endangerment?[30] So we can see that open theism exacerbates the problem of evil, rather than solving it.

Or, on the open-theist view, does God really care more about libertarian freedom than he does about goodness, righteousness, truth, and holiness? Is God willing to risk the loss of goodness in the world in order to give creatures libertarian free will? Scripture certainly suggests otherwise, since it never mentions libertarian freedom, but says much about God's love for what is right and good. And such a view plays into the unbeliever's hands: for the very charge made on the basis of the existence of evil is that the God of theism does not care enough about goodness to prevent evil. On this point, the unbeliever and the open theist agree, and the problem remains.

Indeed, open theists make this problem even worse when they say that God retains the power to intervene coercively in history and that he acts that way when he strongly desires to do something that can't be done with the cooperation of free agents. When the course of history wanders too far away from

---

29. Thanks to Steve Hays for this memorable phraseology.
30. Compare the comments of Nicole, cited in the previous chapter, regarding the enormous risks God took, on the openness theory, and the horrendous miscalculations he evidently made—calling his wisdom and trustworthiness into question.

---

his intentions, he acts unilaterally "to keep things on track."[31] But if God sometimes acts unilaterally to accomplish the things that he desires most, why did he not intervene to prevent the Holocaust? The only answer compatible with open theism is: because he did not care enough.

What, then, is the solution to the problem of evil? I regret that I do not have a fully satisfying answer, but I will make some suggestions to put the issue into perspective:

1. Since Christianity is a revelation from God, one would expect that it would include some things that transcend our understanding—some insoluble mysteries. The problem of evil, I believe, is one of those mysteries. Thus, the existence of the problem of evil is actually a point in favor of the truth of biblical theism.[32]

2. Some theologians seem to be willing to pay any price for a solution to the problem of evil. So open theists insist on libertarianism, a doctrine that is both unscriptural and incoherent, and which actually destroys moral responsibility, as we have seen. And they are even willing to sacrifice God's exhaustive knowledge of the future, another doctrine that, as we shall see, is not biblically negotiable. Would it not be better to leave the problem unsolved than to resort to such drastic measures? Is there no point at which we should be silent and take God at his word? Open theists do not seem to have considered how large a price we should pay to solve this theological problem.

---

31. David Basinger, "Practical Implications," in OG, 159. See Paul K. Helseth's excellent discussion, "On Divine Ambivalence," forthcoming in the *Journal of the Evangelical Theological Society*.

32. Pinnock, as we have seen, thinks that this use of *mystery* is "a euphemism for nonsense." It is sometimes difficult to know when we are stumbling over divine mysteries and when we are merely thinking illogically. But the church has regarded the problem of evil as a mystery since the time of Job. And the argumentation below does at least absolve the traditional view from the charge of irrationality.

3. The transcendence of God plays a significant role in biblical responses to the problem of evil. Because God is the covenant Lord, he is not required to defend himself against charges of injustice. He is the judge, not we. Often in Scripture, when something happens that calls God's goodness into question, he pointedly refrains from giving an explanation. Indeed, he often rebukes those people who question him. Job demands an interview with God, so that he can ask God the reasons for his sufferings (23:1–7; 31:35–37). But when he meets God, God asks the questions: "Brace yourself like a man; I will question you, and you shall answer me" (38:3). The questions mostly reveal Job's ignorance about God's creation: if Job doesn't understand the ways of the animals, how can he presume to call God's motives into question? He doesn't even understand earthly things; how can he presume to debate heavenly things? God is not subject to the ignorant evaluations of his creatures. Job never learns why he has suffered.[33]

Similarly, in Romans 9:19–21, Paul appeals specifically to the difference in metaphysical level and status between the Creator and the creature:

> One of you will say to me: "Then why does God still blame us? For who resists his will?" But who are you, O man, to talk back to God? "Shall what is formed say to him who formed it, 'Why did you make me like this?'" Does not the potter have the right to make out of the same lump of clay some pottery for noble purposes and some for common use?

---

33. The reader knows more than Job himself did about the causes of his suffering, for the reader has access to chapters 1–2, which describe Satan's accusation against Job. But even that passage does not give a thorough account of the reasons for Job's suffering. For the reader also has unanswered questions: Why does God accommodate Satan's challenge in this way? And why does God even permit Satan to enter the heavenly court?

This answer to the problem of evil turns entirely on God's sovereignty. It is as far removed from a freewill defense as one could imagine. Indeed, if Paul believed in libertarian freedom, it is inconceivable that he could have answered the objection in this way.[34]

4. It is also significant to note what God does not say to Job. If God were an open theist, he might say, as Bruce Ware puts it:

> Job, why are you blaming *me* for this suffering? I am not the one behind it! I haven't brought this on you! In fact, I feel as badly about your suffering as you do, and I wish it could have been avoided. Unfortunately, Satan is a very powerful being whose free choices I cannot control, and he has brought on you this suffering. So, stop blaming me for something I have not done and realize that sometimes pointless evil is inflicted on others in a world of sinful creatures who possess moral freedom.[35]

On the open-theist view, that would be the best answer for Job. God could and should tell him something like that. But in fact, he says nothing of the kind. He emphasizes, contrary to open theism, his sovereignty over the whole course of nature and history, so that Job has to confess, "I know that you can do all things; no plan of yours can be thwarted" (Job 42:2).

Indeed, the book of Job leaves no doubt that Job's sufferings came from God (1:21; 42:11).[36] And Paul's argument in

34. Compare other passages in which God rejects challenges to his integrity and turns those charges against his critics: Ezek. 18:25; Matt. 20:1–16; Rom. 3:3–8, 31; 6:1–2, 15; 7:7.

35. Bruce A. Ware, *God's Lesser Glory* (Wheaton, Ill.: Crossway Books, 2000), 201–2.

36. Incredibly, Boyd does not so much as mention either Job 1:21 or Job 42:11 in his *God at War: The Bible and Spiritual Conflict* (Downers Grove, Ill.: InterVarsity Press, 1997), despite the fact that he cites passages from the book of Job sixty times in a substantial discussion on Job and the problem of evil. Thanks to Justin Taylor for this observation.

Romans, as we have seen, ascribes the unbelief of the Jews to the sovereign purpose of God. The uniform witness of Scripture is that the evils of this life come from God. We saw in chapter 5 that God foreordains the worst evil of all, sin, which is at the root of all other evils. So Scripture often speaks of God's foreordination of the consequences of sin (see Ex. 4:11; Deut. 32:39; 1 Sam. 2:6–7; Eccl. 7:13–14; Isa. 45:5–7; Lam. 3:37–38; Amos 3:6). These passages not only speak of particular situations, but ascribe to God all the evils of the world.[37]

5. The passages in Job and Romans are not, of course, the only biblical responses to the problem of evil. Sometimes God does not respond by silencing us, as above, but by showing us in some measure what evil contributes to the goodness of his plan. This has been called "the greater good defense." Scripture does show us many ways in which God brings good out of evil: maturity from chastisement, victory from persecution, glory from suffering. The worst crime in history, the crucifixion of Jesus, brings about the greatest blessing of all time, forgiveness of our sins and eternal fellowship with God. Arguably, we would not have known God's love and mercy to this extent, had God not foreordained the Fall and our redemption.

6. Perhaps even the Cross does not fully explain why God foreordained the Fall. But at least it provides a powerful impetus to faith. If God could bring the greatest good (redemption) out of the greatest evil (the Crucifixion), and in a way that could scarcely be anticipated by human thought, can we not trust him to resolve the remainder of the problem of evil? Can we not believe that a God good enough and powerful enough to bring good from the death of his Son is also

---

37. Open theists will regard this use of texts as "universalizing particulars." They regard these texts as teaching that God foreordains some evils, but not all. My reply here is the same one that I made in chapter 6 in a similar context. Many of these passages emphasize the universality of this principle, and they would lose considerable force if the principle were limited.

good enough and powerful enough to bring good from the Fall itself?

7. Indeed, the promise of Scripture is that he will do so. In heaven, we will no longer grieve over evil. There will be no more tears (Rev. 21:4). All will join in a song of praise, confessing God's justice and truth (Rev. 15:3–4). Do we rejoice because God has revealed a more complete answer to the problem of evil? Possibly. Or does God simply overwhelm us with his righteousness and goodness, thereby putting the remaining mystery in its place? That, I suspect, is more likely.

There is nothing about the problem of evil that requires us to believe in libertarianism. And, as we have seen, there are many reasons not to believe in it. Libertarianism is unscriptural, incoherent, and destructive of both divine sovereignty and human responsibility.

NINE

Is God in Time?

Another important plank in the open-theist platform is the temporality of God. Open theists reject the traditional view that God is supratemporal, "outside" or "above" time. They reject supratemporalism as a product of Greek philosophy rather than Scripture. Indeed, the Greek philosophers Parmenides, Plato, and Plotinus did understand "eternal" reality to be timeless—beyond or outside time—and their teaching may well have influenced Christian thought on the subject. But they did not consider eternity to be the dwelling place of an infinite, personal God.

Theological descriptions of God as timeless, as existing "before"[1] time, and so on, became especially common during the Arian controversy of the fourth century, when orthodox theologians opposed the Arian contention that there was "a time when the Son was not."[2] Athanasius and the

---

1. Strictly speaking, it is improper to speak of something occurring before time, because *before* is itself primarily a temporal expression. Without time, there is no before or after. However, it is convenient for those who believe that time is part of the creation to refer to God's eternal nature apart from creation by the phrase *before time*. There are spatial uses of *before* as well, as in "stand before the king," and perhaps we can think of God "standing before time" in that sort of way.

2. More precisely, the Arians asserted a "when" (*pote*) when the Son was not, rather than a "time" (*chronos*). The difference, in my judgment, is rhetorical rather than substantial.

Nicene Trinitarians insisted that both the Father and the Son existed before time. Time is their creation. So they themselves are essentially timeless.[3] Augustine says to God in his *Confessions:*

> Thy present day does not give way to tomorrow, nor indeed, does it take the place of yesterday. Thy present day is eternity.[4]

The classic statement of God's atemporal eternity is found in Boethius's *Consolation of Philosophy,* 5.6. There he defines God's eternity as "the simultaneous and perfect possession of infinite life." This definition held sway in the church for many centuries. We can find its equivalent in Anselm[5] and Thomas Aquinas[6] (but not in Duns Scotus and William of Occam), and in the major post-Reformation theologies.[7]

The Socinians opposed this view. They held that God's eternity means merely that God has no beginning or end, not that he is above or outside of time itself. On their view, God experiences temporal succession as we do. Their view was a necessary implication of their denial of exhaustive divine foreknowledge.

3. Hilary of Poitiers is a particularly strong example. In *On the Trinity,* 8.40, he says: "Again, let him who holds the Son to have become Son in time and by His Incarnation, learn that through Him are all things and we through Him, and that His timeless Infinity was creating all things before time was."

4. Augustine, *Confessions,* 11.3.

5. Anselm, *Proslogium,* chap. 19, and *Monologium,* chap. 22, in *St. Anselm: Basic Writings,* ed. S. N. Deane (La Salle, Ill.: Open Court, 1962), 25, 78–81.

6. Aquinas, *Summa contra gentiles,* 1. He says (sec. 3): "There is, therefore, no *before* or *after* in Him; He does not have being after non-being, nor non-being after being, nor can any succession be found in his being."

7. Luther and Calvin did not concern themselves much with the definition of eternity, or in general with defining divine attributes. But their successors resumed the discussion, following the Boethian-Augustinian approach, by and large. See Heinrich Heppe, *Reformed Dogmatics* (Grand Rapids: Baker, 1978), 65. Francis Turretin's discussion is representative, in *Institutes of Elenctic Theology* (Phillipsburg, N.J.: P&R Publishing, 1992), 1:202–4.

NO OTHER GOD

In the nineteenth century, some conservative Reformed theologians questioned the Boethian-Augustinian view. James H. Thornwell seemed to be of two minds on the subject. He more or less affirmed the Boethian tradition, but at the same time he commented that "these are abortive efforts to realize in thought what transcends the conditions of our consciousness."[8] The traditional formula, in his view, is a mere negation; it tells us nothing positive about God's eternity, which remains a mystery. Charles Hodge affirmed that all events (past, present, and future) are present to God's mind, but he was agnostic as to whether God experiences temporal succession.[9] The mid-twentieth-century Presbyterian theologian James Oliver Buswell argued that if God is timeless, it is meaningless to say that the elect are predestined before the foundation of the world, and that if the past is not past for God, we are yet in our sins.[10]

Oscar Cullmann argued that "primitive Christianity knows nothing of a timeless God."[11] But James Barr took issue with Cullmann's linguistic arguments.[12]

Others have promoted temporalist positions, such as the philosopher Nicholas Wolterstorff.[13] He argued, first, that productive acts (like creation, providence, and redemption) occurring in time presuppose a temporal cause (in this case, a temporal God). Second, God's redemptive actions in Scripture

---

8. *The Collected Writings of James Henley Thornwell* (reprint, Edinburgh: Banner of Truth, 1974), 1:192.

9. Charles Hodge, *Systematic Theology* (reprint, Grand Rapids: Eerdmans, n.d.), 1:388.

10. J. Oliver Buswell, *A Systematic Theology of the Christian Religion* (Grand Rapids: Zondervan, 1962), 42–47.

11. Oscar Cullmann, *Christ and Time* (Philadelphia: Westminster Press, 1950), 65.

12. James Barr, *Biblical Words for Time* (Naperville, Ill.: Alec R. Allenson, 1969), 67–85.

13. Nicholas Wolterstorff, "God Everlasting," in *God and the Good*, ed. Clifton Orlebeke and Lewis Smedes (Grand Rapids: Eerdmans, 1975), 181–203.

---

are temporally successive, indicating that the biblical writers "regard God as having a time-strand of his own."[14] Third, Wolterstorff argued that unless God is temporal, he cannot know propositions like "event A is happening now," for only a temporal being can know propositions that are temporally "indexed." These arguments, with others, have been accepted by many. So at present one may speak of a consensus among theistic philosophers that God is in time. Joining this consensus are the process theologians and open theists.[15] One vigorous, thorough, and cogent philosophical dissent from this consensus, however, has been written by Paul Helm.[16]

The strongest motive for this consensus, in my opinion, is the desire of these thinkers to make room for libertarian freedom. If God is timelessly eternal, it is difficult to argue that he is ignorant of what to us is future, for he sees all times equally from his eternal vantage point. And if God knows exhaustively what to us is future, then he knows the free acts of human beings before they take place.[17] And if he knows these actions in advance, it is hard to argue that they are free in a libertarian sense.

Not all temporalists, however, are libertarian (let alone open theists), nor are all libertarians temporalists.

Arguments Against Divine Atemporality

Here I shall look at some of the philosophical and theological arguments. We shall look at the biblical data in a later

14. Ibid., 193.
15. Earlier in the twentieth century, the Boston Personalist movement of Edgar Sheffield Brightman and others affirmed divine temporality. Brightman says that "the divine eternity means God's endless duration" in *The Finding of God* (New York: Abingdon Press, 1931), 131.
16. Paul Helm, *Eternal God: a Study of God Without Time* (Oxford: Clarendon Press, 1988).
17. The "before" is, of course, from our temporal point of view.

No Other God

section. The philosophical debates are more complicated than what I present here. I am trying to simplify and compress, to present the gist of the arguments in each case with a summary evaluation.

1. Wolterstorff's first argument above does not persuade me. It is not obvious that an atemporal being could not bring about a series of events in a time sequence without himself being part of the sequence. This argument also suggests that every event presupposes a chain of temporal causes without beginning, an idea that falls prey to the standard criticisms of an "actual infinite." If the chain of causes has no first member, then it has no ultimate cause.

2. Passing over Wolterstorff's second argument for the moment, let us consider his third argument. If God is merely supratemporal, then Wolterstorff is right to say that he cannot know such propositions as "This is happening now." However, my position is that God is not merely supratemporal, not merely transcendent over time, but also immanent in time, just as he is both transcendent over and immanent in the creation as a whole. So, in response to Wolterstorff: (1) God knows all the facts that are expressed by temporal propositions, from his own transcendent point of view, (2) he can know these facts from a human point of view by becoming incarnate, and (3) in one sense, he always knows facts from every finite point of view, because of his immanence in the world.

3. Pinnock and others have argued, further, that if God is supratemporal, then time must be unreal.[18] But surely that does not follow. God is the Creator; the world is his creature. The creature is radically different from the Creator. But it is

18. Clark Pinnock, "God Limits His Knowledge," in *Predestination and Free Will,* ed. David Basinger and Randall Basinger (Downers Grove, Ill.: InterVarsity Press, 1986), 156. See also Paul Helm's discussion of Norman Kretzmann's position in "Timelessness and Foreknowledge," *Mind* 84 (1975): 515–27.

not thereby unreal. God's handiwork is as real as it can be. If God is atemporal, but made time as part of his creation, then time is very much part of the creaturely reality, though not part of the eternal divine reality. This consideration also answers Buswell's argument. The Atonement is really past in the historical sequence that God has made, and the return of Christ is really future, relative to our place in that history.[19] From God's atemporal perspective, our sins are eternally forgiven for Jesus' sake.

4. Another argument is that if God is supratemporal, then all events are simultaneous with each other. Richard Swinburne argues:

> God's timelessness is said to consist in his existing at all moments of human time—simultaneously. Thus he is said to be simultaneously present at (and a witness of) what I did yesterday, what I am doing today, and what I will do tomorrow. But if t1 is simultaneous with t2 and t2 with t3, then t1 is simultaneous with t3. So if the instant at which God knows these things were simultaneous with both yesterday, today and tomorrow, then these days would be simultaneous with each other. So yesterday would be the same day as today and as tomorrow—which is clearly nonsense.[20]

But Helm points out that *simultaneous* is itself a temporal expression. If God is atemporal, then his consciousness is not simultaneous with anything.[21] Swinburne even speaks of "the instant at which God knows these things." But *instant* is also a temporal expression. If God is atemporal, there is no "in-

19. When Buswell says that on the atemporal view God cannot elect people "before" the foundation of the world, atemporalists appropriately reply that some word such as *before* is almost a necessity of language. See the justification for my use of the term in an earlier footnote.

20. Richard Swinburne, *The Coherence of Theism* (Oxford: Clarendon Press, 1977), 220–21.

21. Paul Helm, *Eternal God*, 26–27. He also points out some more complicated issues in this connection, which I must pass by in the present discussion.

No Other God

stant" at which he gains an item of knowledge. He has that knowledge always, from our point of view, and timelessly from his. He looks down on history from his eternal vantage point and sees t1, t2, and t3 as what they are—three different points in the historical sequence.

All of these arguments for God's mere temporality are equally strong as arguments for God's mere spatiality.[22] We could, as in Wolterstorff's first argument, argue that a spaceless, immaterial being cannot create items in spatial relation to one another without himself being in spatial relation to them. Or we could argue that God cannot know that something is "here" without himself having spatial location. Or we could argue that if God is nonspatial, then space must be unreal. If God is aware of locations s1, s2, and s3, we could argue that these locations must be identical with one another. Although many theologians and philosophers want to assert God's mere temporality, relatively few of them (mainly pantheists and panentheists) want to assert his mere spatiality. Perhaps consideration of the similarity of the temporalist arguments with the spatialist arguments will help some to see faults in both.

It is significant that the arguments for divine temporality are largely philosophical. Open theists complain that the arguments for divine supratemporality come from Greek philosophy, but their own arguments are also philosophical. To my knowledge, only Oscar Cullmann and other writers who are dependent on him have tried to make an exegetical case for the temporality of God. And Cullmann's arguments, in view of Barr's reply to them, cannot be taken for granted. So just as temporalists argue that supratemporalism comes from Greek philosophy, so supratemporalists can argue that temporalism comes from modern philosophy. Neither argument refutes the opposing position: it is a genetic fallacy to say that

22. See Paul Helm, "God and Spacelessness," *Philosophy* 55 (1980): 211–21.

a position must be wrong because of its unworthy origins. But the fact that the temporalist position emerges from modern philosophy rather than from Greek philosophy certainly confers no theological advantage on it.

Philosophical Arguments for Divine Supratemporality

As there are philosophical arguments for temporalism, so there are philosophical arguments for supratemporalism. Aquinas, for example, argued that if God were temporal, he could not be unchangeable.[23] Augustine argued that if God were temporal, he would increase in knowledge and therefore be less than omniscient.[24] Boethius's definition of eternity that I cited earlier suggests an argument like this: If God were temporal, he would not possess his entire life all at once. Some of his life experience would be lost to the past, and some would not yet be attainable because it remains in the future. Thus, God would experience lack, contradicting his aseity. And a temporal God would also have his life divided into temporal parts, contrary to the doctrine of divine simplicity.

More recently, W. Norris Clarke has argued that Einstein's discoveries about time refute a temporalist theism, for, on Einstein's view, a point in time is never simply past, present, or future. Pastness, presentness, and futurehood are relative to an observer. If God is temporal, he would be limited to one time frame; if he exists in all time frames, then he is in effect supratemporal.[25]

---

23. Aquinas, *Summa theologica*, 1.10.1; *Summa contra gentiles*, 1.15.3.
24. Augustine, *The City of God*, 11.21.
25. W. Norris Clarke, "Christian Theism and Whiteheadian Process Philosophy: Are They Compatible?" in *Process Theology*, ed. Ronald H. Nash (Grand Rapids: Baker, 1987), 241–42. He also mentions some speculative arguments from the fields of parapsychology and quantum mechanics, from physicist David Bohm and brain researcher Karl Pribham. For a similar argument,

Some have claimed that a God who exists in time, without beginning or end, would embody an "actual infinite," that is, an infinity of actual events in temporal sequence, past and future. If God is temporal, then time is not created. If time is not created, then it extends infinitely far into the past. In that case, an infinity of days would have elapsed before God's creation of the world. But if an infinity of days elapsed before creation, then creation never took place.

These arguments, especially the last two (on relativity and infinity), have some appeal to me, but I am not inclined to put much weight on them. They are essentially speculative, and so they make no demand on a Bible believer.[26]

Scripture on God and Time

As with all theological questions, Scripture alone can ultimately resolve the issue. Cullmann attempted to draw a conclusion on this matter from the New Testament use of *aion* ("age"), the root of the adjective (*aionios*) translated "eternal," found also in phrases like *eis ton aiona* ("forever"). Cullmann thought that because *aion* can designate a finite period of time, *aionios, eis ton aiona,* etc., should not be taken to indicate a timeless realm.[27] Barr, however, replied that the meaning of the adjective and the phrases may be significantly different from that of the noun, and that there is evidence suggesting that these terms were used in a timeless sense.[28] In the Greek philosophical world, as we've seen, *eternity* often has that meaning.

---

see Royce Gordon Gruenler's article in the same volume, "Reflections on a Journey in Process," 348–50, and at much greater length in his book *The Inexhaustible God* (Grand Rapids: Baker, 1983), 75–100.

26. I discuss their merits somewhat in my forthcoming *The Doctrine of God*.
27. Cullmann, *Christ and Time,* 37–50, 61–68.
28. Barr, *Biblical Words for Time,* 82–104.

I agree on the whole with Barr's critique of Cullmann's arguments about *aion* in its various forms. One cannot derive a temporalist view of God from this language. At the same time, the frequent use of *aionios* to refer to the eternal life of God's people should not be taken in an atemporal way. Nothing in Scripture suggests that human beings will ever transcend time.[29] "Eternal" life is life without end, in fellowship with the eternal God. So one would naturally think that the term has the same meaning when applied to God. A number of passages speak of God as having no beginning or end (Deut. 32:40; Pss. 33:11; 93:2; 102:24, 27; 145:13; 146:10), and in the absence of other evidence it would seem best to say only that God is *everlasting:* persisting through time, rather than transcending it.

We should remember, of course, that the biblical writers did not have in mind our modern, scientific concept of time, or even (most likely) the Platonic philosophical distinction between time and eternity. Their understanding of time was more immediate and practical. They understood that God gives us a certain number of years of life before we die, but that his years never fail. There is no reason to suppose that they thought much about the "nature" or "essence" of time, or the relations sustained to time (so defined) by God and man.[30] Certainly they didn't see time primarily as a kind of "box" that a person can be either inside or outside of.

29. Some have taken Rev. 10:6 ("there should be time no longer" KJV) to indicate a nontemporal existence for the creation. But the context speaks rather of impending judgment, so I think the NIV is correct to translate "there will be no more delay." That is the only verse, so far as I know, that has been used to suggest that our eternal life is nontemporal.

30. Ludwig Wittgenstein begins his *Philosophical Investigations* with a quotation from Augustine on the subject. Platonist that he was, Augustine admitted difficulty in defining time: "If nobody asks me, I know; but if somebody asks me, I don't know." Wittgenstein took this as an example of how philosophical problems arise. We use words like *time* very naturally, without perplexity, until some-

So perhaps we should back away a bit from the original terms of our question. It may not be possible to derive from Scripture an explicit answer to the question of whether God is merely temporal or indeed supratemporal. But I do think there is biblical reason to conclude that God's relation to time is very different from our own. For the biblical God transcends a number of limitations associated with our experience of temporality:

1. *The limitation of beginning and end.* In the passages cited above, Scripture teaches that God has no beginning or end. Temporalists and atemporalists agree on that proposition. But it is also significant that the world has a beginning, and that God exists "before" that beginning. Genesis begins with "the beginning" (*reshit, arche*), and many other passages refer to the initial creation as the beginning (e.g., Isa. 40:21; 41:4, 26; 46:10; Matt. 19:4; Heb. 1:10). But the Creator precedes the creation. John 1:1 says that the creative Word existed before the beginning, not only at the beginning. One translation that brings out the durative force of the verb reads, "When all things began, the Word already was."

James Barr argues, contrary to Cullmann, that this beginning can be taken as the beginning of time itself:

> In general there is a considerable likelihood that the early Christians understood the Genesis creation story to imply that the beginning of time was simultaneous with the beginning of the creation of the world, especially since the chronological scheme takes its departure from that date.[31]

body asks us for their "definition" or "essence." Then we are bewildered or "bewitched," and we find it necessary to consult philosophers. Wittgenstein's own suggestion is that if we are able to use the word *time* in its everyday settings, then we understand it sufficiently. It may not be possible to define it, to reduce all its uses to one essence. See Wittgenstein, *Philosophical Investigations* (New York: Macmillan, 1968), 1.

31. Barr, *Biblical Words for Time*, 75.

This "chronological scheme" includes, not only the six days of creation (however they are to be understood), but also the establishment of day and night (Gen. 1:5) and the creation of the heavenly bodies "to separate the day from the night, and let them serve as signs to mark seasons and days and years" (v. 14).

This argument does not prove absolutely from Scripture that time itself had a beginning. It would, of course, be possible for time to exist in the absence of days and nights demarcated by the movements of heavenly bodies. But certainly the biblical writers saw God as having his own existence beyond and prior to the history of the material creation and the human race. And it is problematic to try to imagine what role time would have played prior to the creation, when there were no bodies in motion, but only the unchanging God.[32] What we know as time, measured by the heavens, affecting our practical lives, certainly began with the creation. If God experienced time before the creation, his experience of it was certainly very different from ours today.

2. *The limitation of change.* I have chosen to discuss God's unchangeability at a later point. But clearly God is unchangeable in some respects (Mal. 3:6), and however one interprets it, his unchangeability gives him an experience of time that is different from ours.

3. *The limitation of ignorance.* Over time, our memories of the past grow dim, and our anticipation of the future is always highly fallible. But, as I will argue later, contrary to open theism, God knows perfectly what to us are the past, the present, and the future—seeing them, in effect, with equal vividness. This does not mean that all times are indistinguishable for him. He knows that one event happened on Monday and another on Tuesday, and he understands the process by which one event flows into the next. Thus, it is misleading to say that

32. See my later discussion of God's unchangeability.

there is no succession of moments in God's consciousness.[33] But he does see all events laid out before him, as one can see an entire procession from a high vantage point.

The procession analogy is a frequent illustration of an atemporal consciousness.[34] An atemporal being would see all events equally vividly. Since God can do this, his experience of time, in still another sense, is very different from ours. Indeed, his relationship to time is quite unique.

4. *The limitation of temporal frustration.* To us, time often seems to pass too slowly or too fast. It passes too slowly as we wait for something to happen, but too fast when we face a deadline. For God, however, time never passes too slowly:

> For a thousand years in your sight
>   are like a day that has just gone by,
>   or like a watch in the night. (Ps. 90:4)

But neither does time pass too quickly for God: "With the Lord a day is like a thousand years, and a thousand years are like a day" (2 Peter 3:8). I am not here trying to make a point about time traveling at multiple speeds in God's consciousness. I doubt if these passages have in mind anything so abstruse. Rather, the point is that God is so completely in control of the temporal sequence that he is able to accomplish precisely what he wants.

The same point can be made by reflecting on "when the fulness of the time was come" in Galatians 4:4 KJV ("when the time had fully come," NIV). God has carefully structured

33. God does not sense one moment of his own transcendent consciousness flowing into another. But he fully understands the process by which time flows in the creaturely world.

34. One could also use the analogy of a movie film. When one watches the film projected onto the screen, one watches one frame at a time, each moving into the next. But if one could look at the film itself (only short ones, I gather, are suitable for this illustration), stretched out before one's field of vision, one could see all the frames at once, and therefore all "times" in the film.

---

the whole history of the world to accomplish his own specific purposes, as I argued in chapter 5.

Again, we must conclude that God's experience of time is very different from ours. He looks at time as his tool in accomplishing his purposes; we look at it as a limit on our choices. He is the Lord of time. "By his own authority" he sets "the times or dates" (Acts 1:7; cf. 17:26; Mark 13:32).

What conclusion follows from these four ways in which God transcends limitations associated with time? Shall we say that God is merely "in" time, or is he in some way "outside of" time? Well, try to imagine what it would be like to have a consciousness without beginning and end, without change, with perfect knowledge of all times, and with complete sovereignty over temporal relationships. What would that feel like?

When we talk about ourselves being "in time," part of what we mean is that to us time is a limit. It is a sort of box that we cannot get out of; it limits our knowledge and our choices. To God, time is clearly not that sort of box. A much better metaphor is the atemporalist one, that he looks down on time from a lofty height. So it seems to me that God's experience of time, as Scripture presents it, is more like the atemporalist model than the temporalist one.

I cannot present a watertight argument for divine atemporality. However, it seems to me that once we deny the existence of libertarian freedom, all the relevant considerations favor atemporality, and none favor temporality.

More important than the question of temporality, however, is God's lordship over time. The most common name of God in Scripture is Lord, the regular translation of the mysterious Hebrew name *yahweh* and of the Greek *kyrios*, the regular title of Christ in the New Testament. God's lordship involves his control and authority over all things.[35] His special relationship

35. See my *The Doctrine of God*, chaps. 1–7.

to time, whether temporal or atemporal, should not be defined first in terms of temporality, but in terms of lordship.

Some temporalists have used the phrase "Lord of time" as an alternative to calling God atemporal.[36] But temporalists who espouse libertarian freedom (that is, most temporalists) need to ask how libertarianism can possibly be consistent with divine lordship as Scripture presents it. And once we understand God's lordship in the biblical sense, we will recognize him as Lord of time, and therefore superior to time. In that sense, certainly, his existence is supratemporal. And this supratemporal existence is very much like the picture drawn by Augustine and Boethius: God looking down on the temporal process from an exalted vantage point.

God's Temporal Omnipresence

We have not exhausted the biblical teaching on God's relationship to temporal reality. So far, we have focused on the nature of God's transcendence in relation to time. Now we must look at his temporal immanence.

Here I return to Wolterstorff's second argument, which I passed over earlier, that God's redemptive actions in Scripture are temporally successive, and that the biblical writers regard God as having a time-strand of his own. This is certainly right. I mentioned earlier that God accomplishes his purposes in the fullness of time. That fact is a testimony to his sovereignty, but also to the importance of temporal relationships in the divinely ordained course of history.

The biblical narrative relates a historical succession of events—events of creation, fall, and redemption. As Oscar Cullmann, Geerhardus Vos, and others have pointed out, the

---

36. Cullmann, *Christ and Time*, 69; Wolterstorff, "God Everlasting," 203; Otto Weber, *Foundations of Dogmatics* (Grand Rapids: Eerdmans, 1983), 2:456–58.

New Testament tells us of two ages: the old age and the new age. The old age is the age of fallen humanity, running from the Fall to the Last Judgment. The new age is the age of salvation, beginning with the coming of Christ and running forever into the future. We now live in the time when the two ages overlap. So history is a linear pattern of events, beginning at creation, reaching a climax in the work of Christ, continuing on to the Last Judgment, and concluding in the eternal state.

The work of Christ took place once for all. Its *pastness* is important to the New Testament writers. The *presentness* of the time of decision is also important: "I tell you, now is the time of God's favor, now is the day of salvation" (2 Cor. 6:2). And the *futurity* of the consummation is important: suffering now will be followed by glory later (1 Peter 1:3–7).

All these events are God's works, and so he works in a temporally successive pattern. The sequence is foreordained by God's decree, but he brings it to pass in time. Now Wolterstorff takes this temporal pattern to imply that God has "a time-strand of his own," and therefore that God is temporal.

In one sense, Wolterstorff is correct. God's lordship implies, not only his control of and authority over the world, but also his commitment to the world and his involvement with the course of nature and history. As covenant Lord of Israel, he is committed to Israel, to be their God and be with them as his people (Gen. 17:7; Lev. 26:12; Jer. 7:23; 11:4; 30:22; Ezek. 36:28; 2 Cor. 6:16; Rev. 21:3–4). His covenant presence means both that he is *here* and that he is here *now*. Israel needed to learn in Egypt that God was present, not only to the patriarchs four hundred years before, but to them as well, in their current experience. God not only *works* in time, but is also *present* in time, at all times. His lordship over the universe is analogous. This is his world, made for his purposes. He dwells in and with it, in both time and space.[37]

Too little attention has been paid to God's temporal omnipresence in the discussion of his relationship to time. Much of what some writers want to gain by a temporalist view (other than, of course, libertarian freedom) can be as easily secured through sufficient recognition of God's temporal presence. For example, a present God, like a temporalist God, can know (and assert) temporally indexed expressions like "The sun is rising now." He can feel with human beings the flow of time from one moment to the next. He can react to events in a significant sense (events which, to be sure, he has foreordained). He can mourn one moment and rejoice the next. He can hear and respond to prayer in time. Since God dwells in time, therefore, there is give-and-take between him and human beings.

All Christians acknowledge that in the incarnation of Jesus Christ, the eternal God entered time and experienced to the full the passing of moments and the changes of human life. But in Christ, God entered, not a world that was otherwise strange to him, but a world in which he had been dwelling all along.

But God's temporal immanence does not contradict his lordship over time or the exhaustiveness of his decree. These temporal categories are merely aspects of God's general transcendence and immanence as the Lord. The "give-and-take" between God and the creation requires, not a reduced, but an enhanced, view of God's sovereignty: God is the Lord *in* time as well as the Lord *above* time.

So God is temporal after all, but not merely temporal. He really exists in time, but he also transcends time in such a way as to exist outside it. He is both inside and outside of the temporal box—a box that can neither confine him nor keep him out. That is the model that does the most justice to the biblical data.

37. For a fuller discussion, see my *The Doctrine of God,* chap. 6.

TEN

Does God Change?

Christians have traditionally affirmed that God is immutable, or unchangeable. The doctrine of immutability coheres well with the doctrine of divine supratemporality. Change occurs in and through time; so in God's supratemporal existence, he does not change. We have seen, however, that open theism denies God's supratemporality. So we can understand the open theists' inclination to raise questions also about his immutability.

Pinnock, like other open theists, affirms God's unchangeability in general terms, but he urges us to rethink the concept in its specific applications:

> God is immutable in essence and in his trustworthiness over time, but in other respects God changes. For example, God changes in his response to events in history. The Bible states that when God saw the extent of human wickedness on the earth, he was sorry that he had made humankind (Gen 6:5). The book of Jonah says that when God saw the conversion of Nineveh, he repented of the evil he said he would do to it (Jon 3:10).[1]

1. Clark H. Pinnock, "Systematic Theology," in OG, 117.

Now Scripture does refer to God as unchanging:

In the beginning you laid the foundations of the earth,
   and the heavens are the work of your hands.
They will perish, but you remain;
   they will all wear out like a garment.
Like clothing you will change them
   and they will be discarded.
But you remain the same,
   and your years will never end. (Ps. 102:25–27)

I the LORD do not change. So you, O descendants of Jacob,
are not destroyed. (Mal. 3:6)

Every good and perfect gift is from above, coming down
from the Father of the heavenly lights, who does not change
like shifting shadows. (James 1:17)

One particular emphasis is that God does not break his word
or change his mind:

God is not a man, that he should lie,
   nor a son of man, that he should change his mind.
Does he speak and then not act?
   Does he promise and not fulfill? (Num. 23:19)

He who is the Glory of Israel does not lie or change his
mind; for he is not a man, that he should change his mind.
(1 Sam. 15:29)

In other passages, God says in specific cases that he will not
change his mind (Ps. 110:4, quoted in Heb. 7:21; Jer. 4:28;
15:6; 20:16; Ezek. 24:14; Zech. 8:14–15). So, as we have seen
in earlier chapters, God's counsel stands firm; his purpose will
certainly come to pass (e.g., Deut. 32:39; Ps. 33:11; Isa.
43:13). The image of the rock underscores Yahweh's stability,
the sureness of his purposes.

A God Who Relents

Nevertheless, there are a number of problems that arise in discussions of God's unchangeability. First, as Pinnock points out, there are many passages of Scripture in which God does appear to change his mind. Genesis 6:5 is only one example. In Exodus 32:9–10, God announces judgment against Israel for their false worship:

> "I have seen these people," the LORD said to Moses, "and they are a stiff-necked people. Now leave me alone so that my anger may burn against them and that I may destroy them. Then I will make you into a great nation."

But Moses seeks God's favor, calling on him to "relent" (v. 12). "Relent" here translates *nacham,* the same word translated "change his mind" in Numbers 23:19 and 1 Samuel 15:29 (KJV: "repent").[2] And God does relent: "Then the LORD relented and did not bring on his people the disaster he had threatened" (Ex. 32:14).

Six verses after 1 Samuel 15:29, which denies that God relents, we read:

> Until the day Samuel died, he did not go to see Saul again, though Samuel mourned for him. And the LORD was grieved that he had made Saul king over Israel. (v. 35)

"Was grieved" translates *nacham.* So in this passage we learn that God does not "change his mind" (v. 29), yet he "was grieved" that he had made Saul king (v. 35). These verses appear to be contradictory.

---

2. When used of God, *nacham* of course cannot mean to repent of sin, so the King James translation here is misleading to modern readers. It can mean "relent," "change one's mind," or "be grieved" (usually of an intense grieving).

The prophet Joel calls on Israel to repent:

> Rend your heart
>   and not your garments.
> Return to the LORD your God,
>   for he is gracious and compassionate,
> slow to anger and abounding in love,
>   and he relents from sending calamity.
> Who knows? He may turn and have pity
>   and leave behind a blessing—
> grain offerings and drink offerings
>   for the LORD your God. (Joel 2:13–14)

This passage is especially interesting because it quotes the exposition of the divine name Yahweh in Exodus 34:6–7, but adds to this exposition that the Lord is one who "relents" (*nacham*). (This is evidently an inference from the emphasis on forgiveness in Ex. 34.) So relenting is part of his very nature as the Lord. He is the Lord who relents.

The prophet Amos records a dialogue between himself and the Lord:

> This is what the Sovereign LORD showed me: He was preparing swarms of locusts after the king's share had been harvested and just as the second crop was coming up. When they had stripped the land clean, I cried out, "Sovereign LORD, forgive! How can Jacob survive? He is so small!"
>   So the LORD relented.
>   "This will not happen," the LORD said.
>   This is what the Sovereign LORD showed me: The Sovereign LORD was calling for judgment by fire; it dried up the great deep and devoured the land. Then I cried out, "Sovereign LORD, I beg you, stop! How can Jacob survive? He is so small!"
>   So the LORD relented.
>   "This will not happen either," the Sovereign LORD said. (Amos 7:1–6)

We are reminded here of Abraham's intercession for Lot in Sodom (Gen. 18:16–33) and Moses' calling on God to spare Israel (Ex. 32:9–14). In both passages, the intercessor gets his way. The Lord relents; he retreats from the judgment he originally announced.

When Jonah arrives at Nineveh, he announces: "Forty more days and Nineveh will be overturned" (Jonah 3:4). This is God's word, given through the prophet. But Nineveh is not overturned. God relents from his purpose. Jonah is not surprised, however:

> But Jonah was greatly displeased and became angry. He prayed to the LORD, "O LORD, is this not what I said when I was still at home? That is why I was so quick to flee to Tarshish. I knew that you are a gracious and compassionate God, slow to anger and abounding in love, a God who relents from sending calamity." (4:1–2)[3]

Like Joel, Jonah quotes Exodus 34:6–7, drawing from that passage the conclusion that God relents. This connection with the name Yahweh again suggests that relenting belongs to God's very nature: he is "a God who relents." Relenting is a divine attribute.[4]

But how can this be, in the face of passages like 1 Samuel 15:29, which appear to deny that God relents?

In the light of Joel 2:13–14 and Jonah 4:1–2, it is not a mere game with words to say that relenting is part of God's unchangeable nature. In Jeremiah 18:5–10, God indicates that such relenting is part of his general way of working:

> Then the word of the LORD came to me: "O house of Israel, can I not do with you as this potter does?" declares the LORD. "Like clay in the hand of the potter, so are you in

3. Cf. also 1 Chron. 21:15.
4. The psalmist praises God for his merciful relenting. See Ps. 106:41–45.

my hand, O house of Israel. If at any time I announce that a nation or kingdom is to be uprooted, torn down and destroyed, and if that nation I warned repents of its evil, then I will relent and not inflict on it the disaster I had planned. And if at another time I announce that a nation or kingdom is to be built up and planted, and if it does evil in my sight and does not obey me, then I will reconsider the good I had intended to do for it."

Compare Jeremiah 26:3, 13, 19 (referring to Isa. 38:1–5); 42:10. Here the Lord states that many prophecies of judgment and blessing are *conditional*. God reserves the right to cancel them or reverse them, depending on peoples' response to the prophet. As Calvin puts it, speaking of Jonah's prophecy:

> Who now does not see that it pleased the Lord by such threats to arouse to repentance those whom he was terrifying, that they might escape the judgment they deserved for their sins? If that is true, the nature of the circumstances leads us to recognize a tacit condition in the simple intimation.[5]

Some prophecies, then, may appear to be straightforward predictions, but they are, according to the principle of Jeremiah 18:5–10, really warnings, with tacit conditions attached.

Sometimes, as in the passages from Jeremiah, Joel, and Jonah, those tacit conditions have to do with obedience or disobedience, repentance or complacency. Sometimes, as in Genesis 18:16–33, Exodus 32:9–14, and Amos 7:1–6, prayer is such a condition. When the prophet intercedes for his people, God relents from the judgment he has announced. The prophet stands before the throne of God himself and pleads for God's people, and God answers by relenting.

5. Calvin, *Institutes of the Christian Religion*, 1.17.14.

NO OTHER GOD

How is all of this compatible with the sovereignty of God? Note the following points:

1. Jeremiah 18:5–10 follows a passage (vv. 1–4) in which God compares himself to a potter and Israel to clay. We have seen that, contrary to open theism, this comparison is a radical image of God's sovereignty. God's relenting is his sovereign decision. His right to withdraw his announced judgments and blessings is part of his sovereignty.

2. If we interpret these passages (as did Jonah) according to the principle of Jeremiah 18, we are interpreting them as expressions of his preceptive will, rather than his decretive will:[6] as warnings, not as predictions of what will certainly happen. So there is no question of his decretive will failing. His preceptive will, of course, unlike the decretive, can be disobeyed, though at great cost.

3. Even God's decretive will, his eternal plan, takes human actions and prayers into account. God decrees not only ends, but also means. And he ordains that many of his purposes will be achieved through the means of human prayers and actions. God's decretive will in the book of Jonah is not to judge Nineveh at that time. But he has eternally determined to accomplish his purposes through Jonah's prophecy and the repentance of the Ninevites.[7] It is God's eternal intention to forgive Israel in the situation of Amos 7:1–6. But he does this through the power of Amos's intercession, and not without it.

But how is all this compatible with the authority of the prophetic word? In Jonah 3:4, God through his prophet announces something that does not take place, the destruction of Nineveh. Yet Deuteronomy 18:21–22 says that the test of a true prophet is this:

6. Recall my discussion of this distinction in chapter 7.
7. This is an example of what I mentioned in the previous chapter: the give-and-take between human beings and God in his temporal immanence.

You may say to yourselves, "How can we know when a message has not been spoken by the LORD?" If what a prophet proclaims in the name of the LORD does not take place or come true, that is a message the LORD has not spoken. That prophet has spoken presumptuously. Do not be afraid of him.

On this criterion, should not Jonah have been denounced as a false prophet? No, because God had revealed that such prophecies have tacit conditions. What Jonah said to Nineveh really was, "Yet forty days and Nineveh will be destroyed, *unless* you repent of your sins and turn to the Lord." Jonah himself understood that God might forgive Nineveh (Jonah 4:2), despite the apparently categorical language of the prophecy. The Ninevites understood it, too. Their king said: "Who knows? God may yet relent and with compassion turn from his fierce anger so that we will not perish" (3:9). Jonah was a true prophet, announcing God's judgment with tacit conditions. His words were God's words; his tacit conditions were God's tacit conditions.

But then does Deuteronomy 18:21–22 become a dead letter? Not at all. Not all prophecies are conditional. Sometimes prophets do make straightforward predictions of events to come. Obviously in 1 Samuel 10:1–7, for example, there is no conditionality. Samuel simply tells Saul a number of events that will take place in the immediate future, and they happen exactly as Samuel said. (For other examples, see the general treatment of predestination in chap. 5 and our discussion of divine foreknowledge in chap. 12.) We must determine from the context which principle is operative: straightforward prediction or conditional proclamation.

Some prophecies, moreover, are qualified by assurances. In Jeremiah 7:15, God says that exile is certain—so certain that the prophet is not even to pray for the people, "for I will not listen to you" (v. 16). Here God makes known his decretive will. What he has predicted will certainly come to pass. In Amos 1:3, 6, 9, 13; 2:1, 4, 6, God announces future judgments and says that these will certainly come to pass; he will not turn back his wrath. (For other examples, see Isa. 45:23; Jer. 4:28; 23:20; 30:24; Ezek. 24:14; Zech. 8:14.) Sometimes, indeed, God takes a solemn oath to indicate the certainty of the predicted events (Ps. 110:4; Isa. 14:24; 54:9; 62:8; Jer. 44:26; 49:13; 51:14; Amos 4:2; 6:8; 8:7). Sometimes the phrase "as surely as I live" pledges the unconditional truth of the prophecy (Ezek. 5:11; 14:16, 18, 20; 20:3, 31, 33; 33:27; 35:6, 11). In these examples, God declares his unchangeable decretive will.[8]

We are likely to find tacit conditions in prophecies of blessing and judgment, according to Jeremiah 18:5–10. To be sure, some such prophecies are unconditional, as we saw in the previous paragraph. But most of them are conditional, and most conditional prophecies are prophecies of blessing and judgment. Blessing and judgment are the twin sanctions of God's covenants. Often the prophet serves as the prosecuting attorney for God's "covenant lawsuit." In the covenant, God offers two alternatives: blessing for obedience and cursing for disobedience (e.g., see Deut. 28). It is the prophet's job to hold out both alternatives. Prophecies of blessing and judgment are often conditional because they are proclamations of God's covenant. So it should not surprise us either to find that "relenting" is part of God's covenant name.

To say that much prophecy is conditional is not to say that "anything can happen" following a prophecy. Even conditional prophecy limits what can and cannot happen. The covenant itself is sealed by God's oath, and so its curses and

8. However, the fact that many passages have these explicit assurances suggests that prophecy does not always have this unconditional character. So these passages reinforce our impression that many prophecies in Scripture are conditional.

blessings will certainly come to pass, granted the relevant conditions. The result will not be neutral; it will be either curse or blessing. Most of these prophecies are imprecise, to be sure; they don't describe exactly what kind of blessing or curse is coming, or precisely when. But they speak the truth.[9]

How Is God Unchanging?

We have seen that *unchanging* needs some definition beyond the obvious, since Scripture attributes to God some kinds of changes, even changes of mind. There are also philosophical questions that arise. Say that Susan becomes a Christian on May 1, 1999. Before that date, we could not say of God that he was "believed in by Susan," but after that date we could say that. A change has taken place, one that could be interpreted as a change in God.

Philosophers sometimes call these "Cambridge changes,"[10] to distinguish them from "real changes." On the human level, consider that Mary has the property of being taller than her son Justin on January 1, 1998, but loses that property on January 1, 1999. She has remained the same height, but Justin has grown taller. Normally we would say that Mary has not changed in this respect, but that Justin has. If we are in a philosophical frame of mind, however, we can formulate the event as a change in Mary, by saying that she has lost and/or gained a property. We might call this a Cambridge change as opposed to a real change.

9. In this section, I am greatly indebted to Richard Pratt's important article, "Historical Contingencies and Biblical Predictions," available at www.thirdmill.org. Pratt distinguishes (1) prophecies qualified by conditions, (2) prophecies qualified by assurances, and (3) predictions without qualifications, and he analyzes each group most helpfully.

10. This evidently means that there are some kinds of events that only subtle philosophers would regard as changes.

It is not easy in some cases to distinguish between the two,[11] but most of us would grant intuitively that there is a distinction to be made. Hence, theologians have often said that God does not change "in himself," but does change "in his relations to creatures." When Orlando, Florida, experiences a heat wave, it is not because the sun has grown hotter, but because Orlando stands in a different relation to it. So Herman Bavinck says, "Whatever change there is, is wholly in the creature."[12] When God "changes" his attitude from wrath to favor, it is because the creature has moved from the sphere of Satan to the sphere of Christ.

Some "changes" in God can be understood in this way, but it would be wrong, I think, to understand all of them according to this model. For one thing, Reformed theology insists that when a person moves from the sphere of wrath to that of grace, it is because God has moved him there. God's change in this context (from wrath to grace) is not the product of creaturely change; rather, the creaturely changes come at God's initiative. Pannenberg says that medieval theologians reasoned like this:

> Because of God's immutability any change in God's attitude to sinners has to begin with a change on our side. This was the main impulse behind the development of the Scholastic doctrine of a *gratia creata*. Only when the soul in its creaturely reality is adorned with this grace can the unchanging God have a different attitude toward it.[13]

Certainly the biblical doctrine of God's unchangeability is not intended to lead to such conclusions. But how do we avoid them?

11. See, for example, Paul Helm, *Eternal God* (Oxford: Clarendon Press, 1988), 45.
12. Herman Bavinck, *The Doctrine of God* (Grand Rapids: Baker, 1951), 148.
13. Wolfhart Pannenberg, *Systematic Theology* (Grand Rapids: Eerdmans, 1988), 1:437. He refers to J. Auer, *Die Entwicklung der Gnadenlehre in der Hochscholastik*, vol. 1: *Das Wesen der Gnade* (1942).

I will not take up here the difficult and probably unedifying task of distinguishing Cambridge changes from real changes. If such a distinction turns out to be impossible, then it won't hurt us to concede that God does indeed change in some of these relational ways, just as we have conceded that God changes his mind in some senses. But Scripture does clearly teach that God is immutable in some important ways. So we need to spend some time thinking about what specific changes Scripture intends to exclude when its speaks of God's unchangeability. As I see it, they fall into four categories:

1. God is unchanging *in his essential attributes*. The Westminster Shorter Catechism's answer to question 4 says that "God is a Spirit, infinite, eternal, and unchangeable, in his being, wisdom, power, holiness, justice, goodness, and truth." Hebrews 13:8 (speaking specifically of Christ) and James 1:17 speak in general terms of God being unchangeable. Notice also Hebrews 1:10–12 (quoting Ps. 102:25–27):

> He also says,
> "In the beginning, O Lord, you laid the foundations of
>   the earth,
>   and the heavens are the work of your hands.
> They will perish, but you remain;
>   they will all wear out like a garment.
> You will roll them up like a robe;
>   like a garment they will be changed.
> But you remain the same,
>   and your years will never end."

Here the writer underscores the fundamental contrast between the Creator and the creature: creatures change, but God does not. The passage does not merely say that God is without end, though that is true. Rather, it says that God, unlike nature (which is worn out from one season to the next), always remains the same. And remarkably, the author applies this teaching, not specifically to God the Father, but to Christ. Then in 5:8 he says of Christ, "Although he was a son, he learned obedience from what he suffered." Note the word "although" (*kaiper*). The writer considers it somewhat anomalous that the Son of God should actually suffer and increase in knowledge. (The church deals with that anomaly, of course, by distinguishing between Jesus' divine and human natures.) The author's main conception, therefore, is that God (Father or Son) does not change.

God's wisdom and knowledge are unchanging because, as I shall argue in a later chapter, they are exhaustive. Since God knows all things in all times, from all eternity, his knowledge neither increases nor decreases. Nor does his power change, for God is omnipotent, and there are no degrees of omnipotence. The same must surely be said of God's goodness and truth, for, as we have seen, God is supremely perfect in these attributes—indeed, he is the standard for the corresponding attributes in human beings.

2. God is unchanging *in his decretive will.* Psalm 33:11 reads,

> But the plans of the LORD stand firm forever,
>   the purposes of his heart through all generations.

As we saw in chapters 5–9, God governs all things by the story he has written, his eternal decree that governs the entire course of nature and history. That story has already been written; it cannot and will not be changed.

3. God is unchanging *in his covenant faithfulness.* When God says, "I the LORD do not change. So you, O descendants of Jacob, are not destroyed" (Mal. 3:6), he is telling them that he will surely fulfill his covenant promises, despite Israel's disobedience. He is the Lord of the covenant, and he will not forsake his people. In Micah 7:19–20, the prophet says to God:

You will again have compassion on us;
    you will tread our sins underfoot
    and hurl all our iniquities into the depths of the sea.
You will be true to Jacob,
    and show mercy to Abraham,
as you pledged on oath to our fathers
    in days long ago.

The covenant continues through time. God is present with his covenant people through many generations, despite their temptation to relegate the covenant to a past age. So God says, in Psalm 89:34–37:

I will not violate my covenant
    or alter what my lips have uttered.
Once for all, I have sworn by my holiness—
    and I will not lie to David—
that his line will continue forever
    and his throne endure before me like the sun;
it will be established forever like the moon,
    the faithful witness in the sky.

And God says in Isaiah 54:10,

"Though the mountains be shaken
    and the hills be removed,
yet my unfailing love for you will not be shaken
    nor my covenant of peace be removed,"
    says the LORD, who has compassion on you.

In these contexts, the unchanging character of God's covenant is vitally important to the biblical doctrine of salvation. It is this covenantal immutability that comforts us, that reassures us that as God was with Abraham, Isaac, and Jacob, so he will be with us in Christ. So Jesus is the same, yesterday, today, and forever (Heb. 13:8).

The writer to the Hebrews does say that God's covenant with Israel is "obsolete." Of the new covenant, he says, "By calling this covenant 'new,' he has made the first one obsolete; and what is obsolete and aging will soon disappear" (Heb. 8:13). Does God's covenant, then, change after all? No, the first covenant is obsolete, not because God will violate its terms, but because he will fulfill those terms in a far more glorious manner than the Jews imagined. God's promises endure; through Jesus, all the nations of the earth are blessed:

> Because God wanted to make the unchanging nature of his purpose very clear to the heirs of what was promised, he confirmed it with an oath. God did this so that, by two unchangeable things in which it is impossible for God to lie, we who have fled to take hold of the hope offered to us may be greatly encouraged. We have this hope as an anchor for the soul, firm and secure. It enters the inner sanctuary behind the curtain, where Jesus, who went before us, has entered on our behalf. He has become a high priest forever, in the order of Melchizedek. (Heb. 6:17–20)

4. God is unchanging *in the truth of his revelation.* What God declares to be true was true from the beginning and always will be (Isa. 40:21; 41:4; 43:12; 46:10). So his ancient words remain our infallible guide, despite the passing of time and changes in human culture (Rom. 15:4; 2 Tim. 3:16–17).

Unchangeability and Temporal Omnipresence[14]

These forms of God's unchangeability leave open the possibility that God may be changeable in other respects. We have already seen that God sometimes relents from his announced

---

14. Thanks to Vern Poythress for suggesting to me many of the ideas in this section. I take full responsibility for the formulations.

intentions. How do these changes fit into the overall biblical doctrine of God?

In the previous chapter, I indicated that God exists both above and within time; he is both transcendent and immanent with respect to time. That distinction is relevant to God's unchangeability in important ways. Obviously, God is unchangeable in his atemporal or supratemporal existence. But when he is present in our world of time, he looks at his creation from within and shares the perspectives of his creatures. As God is with me on Monday, he views the events of Sunday as in the past, and the events of Tuesday (which, to be sure, he has foreordained) as future. He continues to be with me as Monday turns into Tuesday. So he views the passing of time as a process, just as we do.

Theologians have sometimes described God's relenting as anthropomorphic. There is some truth in that description, for divine relenting is part of the interaction between God and his people in history, an interaction in which God's activity is closely analogous to human behavior. For example, in the exchange between God and Amos in Amos 7:1–6, God engages in a conversation with a man, as an actor in history. The author of history has written himself into the play as the lead character, and he interacts with other characters, doing what they do.

That is one perspective on the situation. The other is the atemporal perspective: God has eternally decreed that he will forgive Israel, by means of Amos's intercession. This decree never changes.

History involves constant change, and so, as an agent in history, God himself changes. On Monday he wants a certain thing to happen, and on Tuesday he wants something else to happen. He is grieved one day and pleased the next. In my view, this is more than just anthropomorphic description. In these accounts, God is not merely *like* an agent in time; he really *is* in time, changing as others change. And we should not say that his atemporal, changeless existence is more real than his changing existence in time, as the term *anthropomorphic* might suggest. Both are real.

Neither form of existence contradicts the other. God's transcendence never compromises his immanence, nor do his control and authority compromise his covenant presence. God stirs up "one from the east" to subdue nations and kings (Isa. 41:2). This is God as a historical agent. But the prophecy concludes in verse 4:

> Who has done this and carried it through,
>   calling forth the generations from the beginning?
> I, the LORD—with the first of them
>   and with the last—I am he.

God has planned from the beginning that the eastern scourge would devastate Palestine. That is God as an atemporal agent, controlling everything by his decree.

The difference between God's atemporal and historical existences begins, not with the creation of man, but with creation itself. In Genesis 1, God creates light and darkness, and then names them "day" and "night" (v. 5). Here, God is acting in a sequence. Then, on the second day, he makes an expanse to divide the waters, and names it "sky" (v. 8). On the third day, he gathers the sea and lets dry land appear, defining "land" and "seas"—"and God saw that it was good" (v. 10). That last phrase is especially interesting. God acts and then evaluates his own work. He acts and then responds to his own act.[15]

History is like a novel written by God. In a great novel, the author brings about everything that happens, but events can

15. If we take a nonchronological view of the days of Genesis 1, we must still recognize that God's creative work precedes his rest in chronological sequence.

also be explained within the world that the author creates. God's historical novel is a logical, temporal sequence, in which one event arises naturally out of the one before. When God himself becomes an actor in the drama, he acts in accordance with that sequence. He sends the rains and then brings the harvest. At one time, his interest is producing rain; at another, harvest. Thus do his interests change over time, according to his unchanging plan.

So God does change in his immanent, temporal relations with creation. But that fact does not detract in the least from his overall sovereignty. All these changes are the result of his eternal decree, which brings all things to pass, according to his will.

ELEVEN

Does God Suffer?

In chapter 1, I mentioned that Pinnock thinks it important to regard God as "vulnerable." So open theists, along with other recent theologians,[1] take issue with traditional views of God's "impassibility," his immunity from suffering.

As we look at the Scriptures, we need again to make some distinctions and to see this issue in a broader context.

Aseity

Many theologians have regarded God as *a se*, "from himself," meaning that God is self-existent, self-sufficient, self-contained. I believe this description is biblical. God has no needs (Acts 17:25), and so he does not depend on anything

---

1. Of seminal importance is Kayoh Kitamori, *Theology of the Pain of God* (Richmond: John Knox Press, 1965), followed closely by Jürgen Moltmann, *The Crucified God* (London: SCM Press, 1974; San Francisco: HarperSanFrancisco, 1990). Compare Eberhard Jüngel, *God as the Mystery of the World* (Grand Rapids: Eerdmans, 1983), which emphasizes "the identification of God and the crucified Jesus." Feminist theology generally supports this paradigm: e.g., Elizabeth A. Johnson, *She Who Is* (New York: Crossroad, 1996), 246–72. For recent statements of the traditional view, see Richard E. Creel, *Divine Impassibility* (Cambridge: Cambridge University Press, 1986); Millard J. Erickson, *God the Father Almighty* (Grand Rapids: Baker, 1998); Thomas G. Weinandy, *Does God Suffer?* (Notre Dame, Ind.: University of Notre Dame Press, 2000).

outside himself for existence or sustenance. That conclusion follows from my argument in chapters 5–8 that God creates and controls all things by his eternal decree. All things depend on God, not he on them. They are radically contingent; he exists necessarily as God.

Since God is *a se,* no person or thing can threaten his existence or change his essential nature (see the previous chapter). He cannot, therefore, suffer loss to his essential nature. Nor can anything defeat his eternal plan. In those senses, God is incapable of suffering.

Does God Have Feelings?

But there are other kinds of suffering. To feel sadness, for example, is a kind of suffering, and Scripture does ascribe that to God.

Some theologians have pressed the concept of impassibility so far as to deny even that God has emotions. But that view is not biblical. Scripture ascribes many attitudes to God that are generally regarded as emotions, such as compassion, tender mercy, patience, rejoicing, delight, pleasure, pity, love,[2] wrath, and jealousy. I noted in chapter 10 that *nacham* is sometimes properly translated "be grieved" (as of God in Genesis 6:6), and Ephesians 4:30 tells us not to "grieve" the Holy Spirit of God.

Beyond all of that, we should note that God, speaking in Scripture, regularly expresses emotion and appeals to the emotions of his hearers. There is passion in God's words when he addresses Israel: "Turn! Turn from your evil ways! Why will you die, O house of Israel?" (Ezek. 33:11), or when Paul turns from his logical exposition of God's plan of salvation and bursts forth in praise (as, e.g., in Rom. 8:31–39 and 11:33–36).

2. Love is not merely emotional, but it certainly has an emotional component to it.

No Other God

But emotion is present even in language that is relatively calm. That is true of both divine and human language. Calmness itself is an emotion. And even a matter-of-fact statement like "In the beginning God created the heavens and the earth" (Gen. 1:1) is intended, not only to inform us, but to give us a certain feeling about the event described. Indeed, it may not be possible to distinguish the intellectual force of language from its emotional force. Intellectual communication intends to give the hearer, among other things, a feeling of "cognitive rest,"[3] an inner satisfaction that the communication is true.

Scripture does not distinguish "the emotions" as a part of the mind that is radically different from the intellect and the will. It does not specify any metaphysical or categorical difference between feelings, on the one hand, and thoughts and decisions, on the other.

Nevertheless, some theologians have drawn a sharp line between emotions and other kinds of mental content, and they have put biblical references to God's emotions into the category of anthropomorphisms. On this view, for example, when Scripture says that God knows his people, he really does know them, but when it says that God is angry, he is not "really" angry.

Why is it that theologians have sometimes thought that emotions are unworthy of God? D. A. Carson comments:

> In the final analysis, we have to do with the influence of certain strands of Greek metaphysical thought, strands which insist that emotion is dangerous, treacherous, and often evil. Reason must be set against emotion, and vulnerability is a sign of weakness. One may trace this line from Aristotle's "unmoved mover" through platonic and neo-platonic writings to the Stoics. The conclusion must be that "God is sen-

3. See my *The Doctrine of the Knowledge of God* (Phillipsburg, N.J.: Presbyterian and Reformed, 1987), 152–53, in the context of pp. 149–62, and also pp. 335–40.

sible, omnipotent, compassionate, *passionless;* for it is better to be these than not to be" (so Anselm in *Proslogium,* chap. 6).[4]

I think that Carson is right, and that these strands of Greek metaphysical thought are not biblical. So they provide no basis for denying the existence of divine emotions. A few more observations may help to clarify the issue:

1. Emotions in human beings often have physical accompaniments and symptoms: tears, a queasy stomach, an adrenaline flow, etc. Since God is incorporeal, his emotions are not like ours in that respect. Of course, we should not forget that God did become incarnate in Christ, and that Jesus really did weep (Luke 19:41; John 11:35). But God's incorporeality gives us no reason to deny in some general way that God has emotions. In human beings, thinking is also a physical process, involving the brain. But we would never dream of denying that God can think, simply because he is incorporeal.

2. Doctrines like God's eternal decree, his immutability, and his aseity sometimes lead us to think that he cannot truly respond to what happens in the world. Responding seems to assume passivity and change in God. Now emotions are usually responses to events. They are, indeed, sometimes called "passions," a term that suggests passivity. This consideration is one reason why theologians have resisted ascribing emotions to God.

But although God's eternal decree does not change, it does ordain change. It ordains a historical series of events, each of which receives God's evaluation. God evaluates different events in different ways. Those evaluations themselves are fixed in God's eternal plan. But they are genuine evaluations

4. D. A. Carson, *Divine Sovereignty and Human Responsibility* (Atlanta: John Knox Press, 1981), 215.

of the events. It is not wrong to describe them as responses to these events.[5]

Furthermore, we have seen that God is not only transcendent beyond time and space, but also immanent in all times and spaces. From these immanent perspectives, God views each event from within history. As he does, he evaluates each event appropriately, when it happens. Such evaluations are, in the most obvious sense, responses.

Does such responsiveness imply passivity in God? To say so would be highly misleading. God responds (both transcendently and immanently) only to what he has himself ordained.[6] He has chosen to create a world that will often grieve him. So ultimately he is active, rather than passive. Some may want to use the term *impassible* to indicate that fact.

3. As suggested in the second observation, much of what we are inclined to call "emotion" in God is his evaluation of what happens in history. He rejoices in the good and grieves over the evil. There should be no doubt that God, as our supreme authority, is the ultimate and exhaustive evaluator of everything that happens in nature and history. His evaluations are always true and appropriate.

Now sometimes, in order to be appropriate, an evaluation must include some superlatives, some exciting language.[7] For

---

5. Recall again the role I have ascribed to God's knowledge in the very formulation of his eternal plan (chap. 8). God knows what he plans, and each element of his plan takes the others into account. So his eternal plan itself includes his responses to all the elements of that plan.

6. Recall the discussion of God's temporal omnipresence in chapter 10. In Gen. 1, even before man is created, God responds to his own creative actions.

7. I wish this point were better understood by young preachers. Too often they try to convey truth without passion, which often means without making it interesting for the hearers. Sometimes they defend this by saying that they only want to convey the "objective" truth, not mixing it up with "subjective" emotion. But they fail to realize that a dispassionate exposition of God's Word often falsifies it. We do not rightly expound Rom. 11:33–36 unless we somehow convey to our hearers Paul's sense of amazement and wonder. The same point applies to commentators and theologians.

---

example, it is not enough to say merely that God rules; to express the full truth of the matter, we need expressions like "King of kings and Lord of lords." When we find such colorful expressions, we are inclined to say that they express emotion, that they have emotional content. Indeed, they are emotional expressions, but they are also the sober truth. They represent an infallible evaluation of the facts. Again we see a kind of coalescence between emotion and intellect, and an argument in favor of asserting that God has emotions: without emotions, God would lack intellectual capacity, and he would be unable to speak the full truth about himself and the world.

4. Of course, there are emotions that are inappropriate for God. God is never homesick, anxious about tomorrow, inwardly troubled by divided intentions, compulsive, or addicted. He is not like human beings, who are often overcome by waves of passion, who make decisions on the basis of momentary feelings, and whose passions lead them to make false judgments. God doesn't have such kinds of emotions. But that doesn't mean that he doesn't have the emotions ascribed to him in Scripture.

Scripture ascribes grief to God:

> In all their distress he too was distressed,
>   and the angel of his presence saved them.
> In his love and mercy he redeemed them;
>   he lifted them up and carried them
>   all the days of old. (Isa. 63:9)

God is the compassionate God, who knows the agonies of his people, not only as the transcendent author of history, but as the immanent one who is with them here and now. In the incarnate Christ, he draws yet nearer, to be "made like his brothers in every way," in order to be "a merciful and faithful high priest" (Heb. 2:17). So in Christ, we do not have a high priest who is unable to sympathize with our weaknesses, but we have one who has been tempted in every way, just as we are—yet was without sin. (Heb. 4:15)

This emotional empathy can be called "suffering," although that is perhaps a misleading term. There is no reason in these passages to suppose that God suffers any injury or loss. Yet we should take God's grief seriously.

Is God Ever Weak?

Weakness is another form of vulnerability. We may tend to think of God's power as a kind of brute strength that can overpower any obstacle by sheer force. As Paul Helm says:

> It is tempting to think of God as a Herculean figure, able to outlift and out-throw and outrun all his opponents. Such a theology would be one of physical or metaphysical power; whatever his enemies can do God can do it better or more efficiently than they.[8]

But, he adds, we should resist this temptation, "for the Christian view of providence reveals not only the power of God, but his weakness also."[9] How is God weak? Paul says in 1 Corinthians 1:25 that "the weakness of God is stronger than man's strength." He is thinking here of the cross of Christ (see 1:18, 23–24). Jesus was delivered up to death by wicked men, so that God would raise him up in glory, having made him an offering for the sins of his people (Acts 2:23).

Jesus refuses to be an earthly ruler or to bring in his kingdom by the sword. Rather than kill his enemies, he dies at

---

8. Paul Helm, *The Providence of God* (Leicester: InterVarsity Press, 1993), 224. Much of my discussion in this section is based on Helm's, with thanks.
9. Ibid.

---

their hand. All of this gives every appearance of weakness. But Paul says that the cross is "the power of God and the wisdom of God" (1 Cor. 1:24). Clearly, God used this time of weakness to accomplish his most amazing, indeed his most powerful, work, bringing life from death and defeating Satan and all his hosts.

So also in our own time, the most powerful work of God, the gathering of people out of Satan's clutches into Christ's kingdom, is achieved not through warfare or politics, not through the influence of money or fame, but through "the foolishness of what was preached" (1 Cor. 1:21). Jesus sends his people throughout the world, to all nations, bearing only his word (Matt. 28:18–20). But that word is "the power of God for the salvation of everyone who believes" (Rom. 1:16). God's power lies in the humble medium of preaching and indeed in the suffering of his people (1 Peter 2:13–3:22; 4:12–19). They defeat Satan through the armor that God supplies: truth, righteousness, the gospel of peace, faith, salvation, the word of God, and prayer (Eph. 6:10–20). Thus we are "strong in the Lord and in his mighty power" (v. 10).

Open theists, process theologians, and other writers today believe that God is weak in the sense that he is unable to do what he would like to do. On this view, he cannot eradicate evil, though he would like to; and he cannot make much progress without our help. Scripture does not teach the weakness of God in this sense. Indeed, such a view of God contradicts a vast amount of biblical teaching on God's sovereignty, control, and power.

But it is important for us to recognize that God's sovereign, controlling power appears, not only in spectacular displays like the miracles of Jesus, but also in events in which people perceive him as weak. God is at work in ordinary events as much as in extraordinary events. He often works behind the scenes, and he often does his most wonderful works through apparent defeats. So he tells Paul, "My power is made perfect in weakness" (2 Cor. 12:9). And Paul says:

> I will boast all the more gladly about my weaknesses, so that Christ's power may rest on me. That is why, for Christ's sake, I delight in weaknesses, in insults, in hardships, in persecutions, in difficulties. For when I am weak, then I am strong. (2 Cor. 12:9–10)

Does God Suffer Death in Christ?

The form of divine suffering that is most discussed in contemporary theology (see the titles in footnote 1) is the death of Christ. Christians generally recognize in the Atonement the suffering of the Son of God in the flesh. But recently many writers have insisted on also finding there the sufferings of God himself, even God the Father. This is divine vulnerability in the most radical sense.

I agree with Jürgen Moltmann and others that Christ's sufferings are the sufferings of God. The Council of Chalcedon (451), which defined orthodox Christology, said that Jesus has two complete *natures,* divine and human, united in one *person.* We may say that Jesus suffered and died on the cross "according to his human nature," but what suffered was not a "nature," but the person of Jesus. And the person of Jesus is nothing less than the second person of the Trinity, who has taken to himself a human nature. His experiences as a man are truly his experiences, the experiences of God.

Are these experiences only of the Son, and not of the Father? The persons of the Trinity are not divided; rather, the Son is in the Father, and the Father is in the Son (John 10:38; 14:10–11, 20; 17:21). Theologians have called this mutual indwelling *circumcessio* or *circumincessio.*

However, the Father does not have exactly the same experiences of suffering and death that the Son has. Although they dwell in one another, the Father and the Son play different roles in the history of redemption. The Son was baptized by John; the Father was the voice from heaven at his baptism. The Son was crucified; the Father was not. Indeed, during the Crucifixion, the Father forsook the Son as he bore the sins of his people (Matt. 27:46). Was the Father, nevertheless, still "in" the Son at that moment of separation? What exactly does it mean for the Father to be "in" the Son when he addresses the Son from heaven? These are difficult questions, and I have not heard any persuasive answers to them. But we must do justice to both the continuity and the discontinuity between the persons of the Trinity. Certainly the Father empathized, agonized, and grieved over the death of his Son, but he did not experience death in the same way that the Son did.

But God the Son did die, and of course he rose again. So in his incarnate existence, God suffered and even died—yet his death did not leave us with a godless universe. Beyond that, I think we are largely ignorant, and we should admit that ignorance.

To summarize, let us distinguish between four modes of divine existence:

1. In his atemporal and nonspatial transcendent existence, God ordains grievous events and evaluates them appropriately. He grieves in that sense, but does not suffer injury or loss.

2. In his temporal and spatial omnipresence, he grieves with his creatures, and he undergoes temporary defeats on his way to the complete victory he has foreordained. He is distressed when his people are distressed (Isa. 63:9), but he promises complete victory and vindication both for himself and for his faithful ones.

3. In the Incarnation, the Son suffers injury and loss: physical pain, deprivation, and death. The Father knows this agony, including the agony of his own separation from his Son. He regards this event as the unique and awful tragedy

that it is, but also as his foreordained means of salvation. What precise feelings does he experience? We do not know, and we would be wise not to speculate. But surely, as he is afflicted in Israel's afflictions, he is afflicted in the afflictions of his Son.

So in Jesus, God does share our sufferings in order to overcome them:

> He was despised and rejected by men,
>   a man of sorrows, and familiar with suffering.
> Like one from whom men hide their faces
>   he was despised, and we esteemed him not.
> Surely he took up our infirmities
>   and carried our sorrows,
> yet we considered him stricken by God,
>   smitten by him, and afflicted. (Isa. 53:3–4)

As we have seen from Hebrews, Christ was made like us so that he could be a merciful and faithful high priest, empathizing with our infirmities. He takes away sin, the cause of those infirmities, and he hears our prayers with understanding. But this principle should not be magnified, as it is in open theism, into a metaphysical assertion about God's vulnerability, for, as we have seen, God's eternal nature is invulnerable, and that invulnerability is also precious to the believer.

God's suffering love in Christ, therefore, does not cast doubt upon his aseity and unchangeability. It is, however, ground for rejoicing. I close with words of B. B. Warfield:

> We have a God who is capable of self-sacrifice for us. . . .
> Now, herein is a wonderful thing. Men tell us that God is,
> by very necessity of His nature, incapable of passion, inca-
> pable of being moved by inducement from without; that he
> dwells in holy calm and unchangeable blessedness, un-
> touched by human sufferings or human sorrows for ever,—
> haunting

The lucid interspace of world and world,
Where never creeps a cloud, nor moves a wind,
Nor ever falls the least white star of snow,
Nor ever lowest roll of thunder moans,
Nor sound of human sorrow mounts to mar
His sacred, everlasting calm.

Let us bless our God that it is not true. God can feel; God
does love. We have Scriptural warrant for believing, as it has
been perhaps somewhat inadequately but not misleadingly
phrased, that moral heroism has a place within the sphere
of the divine nature: we have Scriptural warrant for believing that, like the hero of Zurich, God has reached out loving arms and gathered to his own bosom that forest of
spears which otherwise had pierced ours.

But is not this gross anthropomorphism? We are careless
of names: it is the truth of God. And we decline to yield up
the God of the Bible and the God of our hearts to any
philosophical abstraction. We have and we must have an
ethical God; a God whom we can love, in whom we can
trust.[10]

---

10. B. B. Warfield, "Imitating the Incarnation," a sermon on Philippians
2:5–8, in B. B. Warfield, *The Person and Work of Christ* (Philadelphia: Presbyterian
and Reformed, 1950), 570–71. Thanks to Jeff Meyers for drawing my attention
to this passage.

Does God Know Everything in Advance?

Perhaps the best-known assertion of open theists is that God does not know the future exhaustively. In their view, God is often ignorant of what will happen,[1] and sometimes even mistaken.[2] He "expresses frustration"[3] when people do things that he has not anticipated. He changes his mind when things don't go as he had hoped.[4] In these contentions, open theists admittedly differ from "the classical view of God worked out in the Western tradition,"[5] which prevailed from the time of the early church fathers down to the present, with a few exceptions (such as the Socinian heresy).[6] This classical view has been the position of all Christian theological traditions: Eastern Orthodox, Roman Catholic, and Protestant.[7]

---

1. Clark H. Pinnock, "Systematic Theology," in OG, 121–24.
2. John Sanders, *The God Who Risks* (Downers Grove, Ill.: InterVarsity Press, 1998), 132–33.
3. Pinnock, "Systematic Theology," 122.
4. Richard Rice, "Biblical Support for a New Perspective," in OG, 26–35.
5. John Sanders, "Historical Considerations," in OG, 59.
6. See the references to Socinianism in chapter 2.
7. Gregory A. Boyd, in *God of the Possible* (Grand Rapids: Baker, 2000), 116, says, "No ecumenical creed of the orthodox church has ever included an article

It affirms that God has complete knowledge of all events in the past, present, and future. Thus, open theism denies the historic Christian view of God's omniscience.

Open theism's view of God's omniscience is an implication of its libertarian view of human freedom, which I discussed in chapter 8. If people are free in the libertarian sense, then human decisions are radically unpredictable. Even God cannot know them in advance. If in 1930 God knew that I would be writing this book in 2000, then I would not be writing it freely. I could not avoid writing it. So if my writing is a free choice in the libertarian sense, then not even God could have been certain of it in advance. Libertarian freedom excludes the classical view of God's foreknowledge.[8] Pinnock says:

> However, omniscience need not mean exhaustive foreknowledge of all future events. If that were its meaning, the future would be fixed and determined, much as is the past. Total knowledge of the future would imply a fixity of events. Nothing in the future would need to be decided. It also would imply that human freedom is an illusion, that we make no difference and are not responsible.[9]

---

of faith on divine foreknowledge," implying that the whole matter is an open question for Christianity. If by "ecumenical" creed we mean creeds like the Apostles' Creed and the Nicene Creed, which are accepted by all branches of Christianity, then Boyd here makes a correct historical observation. But those ecumenical creeds are rather brief. They don't include articles on justification, for example. If we move ahead to the Reformation period, however, we encounter the Westminster Confession of Faith, which says that "in [God's] sight all things are open and manifest, His knowledge is infinite, infallible, and independent upon the creature, so as nothing is to Him contingent, or uncertain" (2.2), and the Confession reinforces this understanding of God's knowledge with its position on God's decree (chap. 3), creation (chap. 4), providence (chap. 5), free will (chap. 9), and effectual calling (chap. 10). For the Reformed tradition, at least, the extent of God's foreknowledge is not an open question.

8. Traditional Arminianism tries to hold onto both libertarianism and exhaustive divine foreknowledge. In this respect, open theism is more logical than traditional Arminianism, but it pays a high theological price for its superior logic.

9. Pinnock, "Systematic Theology," 121.

He is saying that God cannot know the future exhaustively, because if he did, we would not have libertarian freedom.

On this view, the future is of such a nature that it cannot be known exhaustively. Open theists claim that God is indeed omniscient, but only in the sense that he knows everything that can be known. That he lacks exhaustive knowledge of the future is no more of a limitation than his inability to make a square circle. Just as his omnipotence enables him to do everything that can be done, so his omniscience enables him to know everything that can be known. That includes knowledge of the past and present, but not the future, so open theists name their view *presentism*.[10]

In chapter 8 of this book, however, I argued that libertarianism is both unscriptural and incoherent. Therefore, it provides no barrier to our confession that God knows the future exhaustively. But libertarianism is so important to the open-theist position that without it, the entire position lacks credibility.

Divine Ignorance in Scripture?

Nevertheless, we should consider the open-theist contention that Scripture itself reveals a God who is sometimes ignorant of the future. Pinnock says:

> Many believe that the Bible says that God has exhaustive foreknowledge, but it does not. It says, for example, that God tested Abraham to see what he would do and after the test says through the angel, "Now I know that you fear God" (Gen 22:12). This was a piece of information God was eager to secure. In another place Moses said that God was testing the people in order to know whether they actually love him or not (Deut 13:3).[11]

10. Sanders, *The God Who Risks*, 198–99.
11. Pinnock, "Systematic Theology," 121–22.

He also mentions Jeremiah 32:35 ("nor did it enter my mind, that they should do such a detestable thing") and the verses in which God hopes that "perhaps" his people will listen (e.g., Jer. 26:3; Ezek. 12:3). In this discussion, Pinnock talks several times about the importance of libertarian freedom, which makes one ask if he is reading these texts through a libertarian lens.[12]

As I indicated earlier, other open theists also discuss passages in which, on their view, God is uncertain, changes his mind, is frustrated, discovers new information, and so on. In this book, I cannot deal exhaustively with this list of passages, but I will suggest some principles that bear on their interpretation:[13]

1. Typically, passages in which God "finds out" something occur in judicial contexts. In Genesis 3:9, God asks Adam, "Where are you?" This is not a request for information.[14] Rather, in this verse God begins his judicial cross-examination. Adam's responses will confirm God's indictment, and God will respond in judgment and grace. Similarly, other texts where God "comes down" to "find out" something occur in a judicial context (see Gen. 11:5; 18:20–21;[15] 22:12;[16] Deut. 13:3; Pss. 44:21; 139:1, 23–24). When God draws near, he draws near as the judge. He conducts a "finding of fact" by personal observation and interrogation, and then renders his

12. Ibid., 122–23.
13. For a more thorough discussion, see my forthcoming *The Doctrine of God*, especially chap. 22.
14. If it were such a request, it would show God's ignorance of the present, not the future. But open theists usually accept that God knows the present exhaustively.
15. If, in Gen. 3:9, 11:5, and 18:20–21, God's "finding" presupposes his ignorance, then it is ignorance of the present, not only of the future. But if Gen. 11:5 and 18:20–21 can be explained without assuming divine ignorance, then the same is certainly true of the other passages.
16. Gen. 22:14 also speaks of God's knowledge of the present, rather than of the future. On the open-theist rendering, we would have to conclude that before Abraham's journey, God did not know whether Abraham feared him. In other words, God was ignorant as to the state of Abraham's heart in the present.

verdict and sentence (often, of course, mitigated by his mercy). So not one of these passages entails divine ignorance.

2. God's "remembering" and "forgetting" are also judicial categories in Scripture, because they are covenant categories. When God "remembers" his covenant, he is simply carrying out its terms. So God "remembered" Noah and the earth's creatures in Genesis 8:1 (cf. 9:15–16; Ex. 6:5).[17] God's "forgetting" is either his delay in fulfilling the covenant's terms (Pss. 9:18; 13:1) or his administration of the curse to covenant breakers (Jer. 23:39).

3. When God says that something did not "enter my mind" (Jer. 7:31; 19:5; 32:35), he is not confessing ignorance, but describing his standards for human behavior (still another judicial point). Note the context of Jeremiah 7:31:

> They have built the high places of Topheth in the Valley of Ben Hinnom to burn their sons and daughters in the fire—something I did not command, nor did it enter my mind.

The contexts of 19:5 and 32:35 are similar. "Mind" here is *heart* in Hebrew, which often in Scripture is the locus of intentions (cf. 2 Chron. 7:11; Neh. 7:5). God is saying here that horrible human sacrifices are utterly contrary to his holy standards. God was not at all ignorant of these practices or of the danger that Israel would be tempted to sin in this way. He explicitly forbade human sacrifice in Leviticus 18:21 and

---

17. Douglas Wilson comments on Gen. 8:1 ("But God remembered Noah"): "Does God smack his forehead in this passage? 'Oh, yeah! *Noah!*' Or in Ex. 6:5: 'Man, that was close! I almost forgot. The *covenant!*'" See Wilson, *Knowledge, Foreknowledge, and the Gospel* (Moscow, Ida.: Canon Press, 1997), 39. Neither Sanders nor Boyd, in the books previously cited, includes Gen. 8:1 or Ex. 6:5 in his Scripture index. Sanders (but not Boyd) describes the rainbow of Gen. 9:14–16 as God's "reminder to himself," suggesting at least that God might otherwise have forgotten his plan. But such an idea impugns, not God's knowledge of the future, but his knowledge of the past, despite the open theists' affirmations that God's knowledge of the past is exhaustive.

Deuteronomy 18:10. So, in the intellectual sense, these practices did enter his mind.

4. Some passages do say that God changes his mind in response to circumstances. This is the divine relenting that I discussed in chapter 10. God's relenting is based on his eternal plan, which incorporates his appropriate responses to events in the created world. It implies no ignorance about the future. Sometimes God's announcements of judgment are conditional, to be rescinded if met by repentance. But surely God can make a conditional announcement without being ignorant of anything. These announcements are not declarations of God's eternal purpose, so their conditionality does not imply that God's purpose can change.

5. In another group of passages, God seems to confess his ignorance of future events. In the wake of Israel's idolatry, he says, "I thought that after she had done all this she would return to me but she did not" (Jer. 3:6–7; cf. vv. 19–20).[18] Compare also the use of "perhaps" in Jeremiah 26:3; 36:3; 36:7 and Ezekiel 12:3. If the future is settled to God, how can he speak with apparent uncertainly about what "perhaps" may happen?

In Jeremiah 3, God interacts with Israel as a husband with his unfaithful wife. As in the "relenting" passages discussed in chapter 10, this passage deals with God's relation to Israel in history, not his eternal decrees and eternal foreknowledge. The thrust of the passage is that recent history should have motivated the repentance of Israel and Judah, but in fact they continued their spiritual adultery. As their husband, God had hoped (this hope being an expression of his preceptive will) for something better. But their continuing unrepentant idol-

18. Others have translated this passage in such a way as to create no problem for divine knowledge. The KJV of verse 7 reads, "And I said after she had done all these things, Turn thou unto me. But she returned not. And her treacherous sister Judah saw it."

atry led to his verdict (a judicial verdict, in effect, as in the passages discussed earlier). Nevertheless, we are amazed to see that he still calls upon them to return to him and gives promises of blessing (vv. 14–25).

God is certainly not surprised by Israel's idolatry. Israel bowed to a golden calf in Exodus 32, and God anticipates Israel's continuing idolatry in Deuteronomy 31:16–21 and 32.

In the "perhaps" passages like Jeremiah 26:3, God is telling Israel that her idolatry is utterly unreasonable, both in view of his previous revelation to them (Jer. 26:3; 36:3) and in view of past events.[19] As in Isaiah 5:1–7, God has done things for Israel that should have motivated repentance. But Israel has not responded, exposing the willfulness and persistence of her sin. In other words, God has acted to lessen the probability of Israel's sin, and objectively he has indeed lessened it. He expresses the objectivity of that probability strongly: as a divine thought. But that divine thought is of a probability, not a certainty. God knew all along that Israel would respond as she did.

So understood, these passages are similar to the passages described under the first point above. For the contexts here are essentially judicial. God gives to Israel enormous advantages of revelation and blessing, blessings that should be sufficient to motivate repentance, but she refuses. Thus, as with Abraham in Genesis 22, God "finds out" what is in Israel's heart. On that basis, God draws up an indictment to bring against his people. Until that indictment, there is uncertainty, not in God's mind, but as to Israel's legal status before him within the covenant.

Open theists will complain that I am not reading these passages straightforwardly. But on that question see my discus-

19. The point of Jer. 3:6–7 seems to be that Israel, after committing so much idolatry, should have returned to the Lord, if only for a change of pace! But even that motive didn't bring her back to the Lord.

sion in chapter 3. I am at this point acknowledging anthropomorphism in a stronger sense than I have elsewhere in this book. But surely my reading of these passages is no more anthropomorphic than common exegeses of passages in which God speaks of his hands and eyes. And in view of the overall teaching of Scripture, certainly this level of anthropomorphism is justified.

6. Open theists sometimes suggest that because God changes in his relationships to creatures over time, the future cannot be settled and knowable. God responds to creatures, they say, so he awaits their decisions. He doesn't know in advance what they or he will do. Now I argued in chapter 9 that God does respond to creatures in his temporal omnipresence. But I pointed out that this divine responsiveness is not incompatible with a settled, knowable future. God has foreordained the future, and his eternal plan includes all the actions of creatures, as well as his responses to those actions.

So God is both fully omniscient and responsive to creatures. We may be grateful to the open theists for showing how pervasive in Scripture is the theme of divine responsiveness. But our conclusion should not be to deny God's exhaustive sovereignty and foreknowledge. Rather, we should see him as even more sovereign than we had thought before: ruling not only from a timeless, transcendent realm, but also as temporally omnipresent, existing in and with all the changing events of nature and history, using the give-and-take of history to accomplish his unchangeable eternal purpose, ruling immanently as the Lord.

God's Exhaustive Knowledge of the Future

We have seen, therefore, that God's responsiveness noted in Scripture does not refute belief in his eternal decree and exhaustive foreknowledge. But does Scripture give positive testimony to God's exhaustive foreknowledge?

Scripture typically shows us God's knowledge of the future by the phenomenon of prophecy. One aspect of prophecy is the prediction of future events. Indeed, one test of a true prophet is that his predictions must come true (Deut. 18:22). In Isaiah, God challenges the gods of the other nations to foretell the future, knowing that only he is able to do this (Isa. 41:21–23; 42:9; 43:9–12; 44:7; 46:10; 48:3–7).

Open theists agree that there is a predictive element in prophecy, but they insist that this predictive element does not imply that God has exhaustive foreknowledge. To show this, Rice enumerates three types of prophecy:

> A prophecy may express God's intention to do something in the future irrespective of creaturely decision. If God's will is the only condition required for something to happen, if human cooperation is not involved, then God can unilaterally guarantee its fulfillment, and he can announce it ahead of time. . . .
>
> A prophecy may also express God's knowledge that something will happen because the necessary conditions for it have been fulfilled and nothing could conceivably prevent it. By the time God foretold Pharaoh's behavior to Moses, the ruler's character may have been so rigid that it was entirely predictable. . . .
>
> A prophecy may also express what God intends to do *if* certain conditions obtain.[20]

I agree that in Scripture there are prophecies of these three kinds. I discussed conditional prophecies earlier, and of course I concede that God can announce his own actions that are independent of creaturely decision.[21] The second kind of

20. Rice, "Biblical Support for a New Perspective," 51.
21. I would make two comments, however, about this kind of announcement: (1) Creaturely decisions are themselves the result of God's decisions. So God's decisions are always independent of creaturely decisions in an important sense. (2) On an open-theist view, many of God's own decisions are responses to free decisions of human beings. But if God cannot know human free deci-

prophecy that Rice mentions ought to be troubling to open theists, because (as I mentioned earlier with regard to Boyd's interpretation of Judas) it suggests that some human decisions (Pharaoh's, in the quote from Rice) are morally responsible, even though they are clearly not free in the libertarian sense. It is odd to see open theists speaking of "necessary conditions" for someone's behavior and using terms like "rigid" and "entirely predictable"—deterministic language used in support of a libertarian view of things! Of course, for open theists, Pharaoh and Judas hardened themselves before their hardening became irreversible—that is, before God hardened them. Nevertheless, even the open theists must admit that once their hardening had taken place, God held them responsible for actions they could not have avoided.

However, there are other prophecies that (1) do not merely state divine intentions, but depend for their fulfillment on human choices, (2) imply that God's decision determines those human choices, and (3) are not merely conditional.

Consider, for example, the early prophecies of the history of God's people, given by God to Noah (Gen. 9:26–27), Abraham (Gen. 15:13–16), Isaac (Gen. 27:27–29, 39–40), Jacob (Gen. 49:1–28), Balaam (Num. 23–24), and Moses (Deut. 32:1–43; 33:1–29). Here God announces (categorically, not conditionally), many centuries ahead of time, the character and history of the patriarchs and their descendants. These prophecies anticipate countless free decisions of human beings, long before any of them have the opportunity to form their own character.

---

sions in advance, how does he know what he himself will do? Most every event in the world depends to some extent on human decisions. Natural disasters are the result of the Fall. Wars, human deaths, the rise and fall of kingdoms, the birth of Jesus, his death, the success of the church's preaching: all these things are the result of human free decisions. If God cannot know any of these free decisions in advance, how can he know how he will respond to them?

In 1 Samuel 10:1–7, the prophet Samuel tells King Saul that after he leaves Samuel, he will meet two men, and then three men, and later a group of prophets. Samuel tells him precise details of the trip. Clearly here God through Samuel anticipates in detail the free decisions of the men involved, as well as the events of the journey. Compare a similarly detailed account of an enemy's war movements in Jeremiah 37:6–11.

In 1 Kings 13:1–4, God through a prophet tells wicked King Jeroboam that he will raise up a faithful king, Josiah by name. This prophecy was given three hundred years before the birth of King Josiah. Compare the references in Isaiah 44:28–45:13 to the Persian King Cyrus over one hundred years before his birth.[22] Many marriages, many combinations of sperm and egg, many human decisions were necessary in order for these precise individuals to be conceived, born, and raised to the throne to fulfill these prophecies. These texts assume that God knows how all these contingencies will be fulfilled. The same is true of Jeremiah 1:5, in which God knows Jeremiah before he is in the womb and appoints him as a prophet. Compare also the conversation between Elisha and the Syrian Hazael in 2 Kings 8:12, and the detailed future chronology of the affairs of empires and the coming of the Messiah in Daniel 9:20–27.

In Matthew 26:34, Jesus tells Peter that before the cock crows, Peter will deny him three times. Boyd's explanation is extremely implausible:

> We only need to believe that God the Father knew and revealed to Jesus one very predictable aspect of Peter's character. Anyone who knew Peter's character perfectly could have predicted that under certain highly pressured cir-

---

22. I am assuming, of course, that Scripture is accurate in its account of when these events took place. If Scripture is God's Word, then we must assume such accuracy, contrary to the usual approach of liberal Bible critics.

cumstances (that God could easily orchestrate) he would act just the way he did.[23]

Are we to suppose that Peter's character was so firmly fixed that he would deny Jesus exactly three times and would not wait for the cock to crow before he did so?[24] Surely this prediction is better explained simply by the fact that God has supernatural and exhaustive knowledge of the future, including all the free decisions of human beings.

Scripture is not unclear as to how God gets this extraordinary knowledge. He knows it because, as I argued in chapter 5, he controls all the events of nature and history by his own wise plan. God has made everything according to his wisdom (Ps. 104:24), and he works out everything in conformity with the purpose of his will (Eph. 1:11). Therefore, God knows all about the starry heavens (Gen. 15:5; Ps. 147:4; Isa. 40:26; Jer. 33:22) and all about the tiniest details of the natural world (Pss. 50:10–11; 56:8; Matt. 10:30). "God knows" is an oath-like utterance (2 Cor. 11:11; 12:2–3) that certifies the truth of human words on the assumption that God's knowledge is exhaustive, universal, and infallible. God's knowledge is absolute and perfect, and so it elicits praise (Ps. 139:17–18; Isa. 40:28; Rom. 11:33–36).

So God "knows everything" (1 John 3:20). And,

> nothing in all creation is hidden from God's sight. Everything is uncovered and laid bare before the eyes of him to whom we must give account. (Heb. 4:13)

23. Boyd, *God of the Possible*, 35.
24. Another problem with Boyd's analysis has to do with the "orchestration" he attributes to God. As elsewhere, Boyd recognizes here an occasion when God in effect controls a man's free choice. And, contrary to libertarianism, I presume, Boyd shares Peter's judgment that he was responsible for his action, even though it was not "genuinely free."

Does that knowledge include exhaustive knowledge of the future? Given the inadequacy of the open-theist arguments, the strong emphasis in Scripture on God's unique knowledge of the future, and the biblical teaching that God's plan encompasses all of history, we must say yes.

THIRTEEN

Is Open Theism Consistent with Other Biblical Doctrines?

In this book, I have focused on the open-theist view of God. But because of the importance of the doctrine of God in the Christian faith, errors in that doctrine are likely to affect other areas of doctrine as well. I will not discuss these other areas in detail, but to get a complete picture of open theism, we must get at least an outline of the larger picture.[1] I am not charging every open theist with every error listed in this chapter. For the most part, I see this chapter as setting forth the logical implications of open theism, rather than the actual teachings of its proponents. But I do think that these implications indicate grave dangers in the movement.

Biblical Inspiration

Open theism, like Arminianism, faces the question of how God can inspire a sacred text using human authors, when

---

1. In this chapter, I am much indebted (even more so than in previous chapters) to Roger Nicole's "A Response to Gregory A. Boyd's *God of the Possible*" (publication forthcoming).

those authors are free in a libertarian sense. On such a view, God cannot guarantee the truthfulness of the written Word without overriding the free will of those human writers. Freewill theism, therefore, encourages either a denial of inspiration or a view in which God manipulates the human writers in mechanical fashion. Ironically, freewill theism, which so cherishes the spontaneity of human action, must deny it in this instance, if it wishes to maintain a traditional (and, to my mind, biblical) view of scriptural authority.

Even more seriously, open theism implicitly questions, not only the traditional view of the human authors, but of the divine author as well. For in open theism, God himself is unable to speak with absolute authority. He is ignorant of many future events, which makes him unsuited for the work of prophecy. Furthermore, as we have seen, even his knowledge of the past and the present is problematic in open theism. God is ignorant, for example, of the state of Abraham's heart in the past and present (Gen. 22). We wonder, too, whether the open-theist God is also ignorant of natural phenomena, since on Sanders's account God does not control all the weather (chap. 6).

Even worse, because of his ignorance, the open-theist God sometimes gives bad advice. According to Boyd, God may give guidance to someone that turns out to be bad advice. To Boyd, God is not to blame, because he could not have anticipated the turn of events. He made his best judgment, but that turned out to be faulty.[2] So even God, it would seem, is unable to produce a written text that would give infallible guidance to people. If open theists believe in an authoritative, inspired Bible, that belief would seem to be a happy inconsistency within their overall system.

2. See Gregory A. Boyd's (now notorious) discussion of the experience of "Suzanne," in *God of the Possible* (Grand Rapids: Baker, 2000), 103–6.

No Other God

Open theists almost never formulate doctrines of biblical authority, let alone inerrancy. And they almost never include references to biblical scholars who maintain the inerrancy of Scripture.

Sin

The doctrine of libertarian freedom has always been difficult to reconcile with the biblical doctrine of original sin. For that doctrine states that we are guilty of the sin of Adam. But libertarians tend to believe that we are guilty only of those sins that we have committed "freely," on their definition of "free." As I argued in chapter 8, this view of freedom actually destroys moral responsibility and therefore any orthodox view of human sinfulness. Certainly it is not compatible with the doctrine of original sin as taught in the Reformation confessions.

Redemption

Just as the doctrine of original sin is incompatible with libertarianism, so is the doctrine of imputed righteousness. How can God accept me as righteous, simply on the basis of the righteousness of Christ? On a libertarian basis, no one is righteous unless he performs righteous acts that are freely chosen.

So some of the open theists seek, as part of their "new model" of theology, to minimize or avoid the legal and forensic aspects of salvation. On this view, Jesus did not die to satisfy divine justice, but merely to provide a demonstration of divine love—what has been called the "moral influence" view of the Atonement.[3] In their view, reconciliation does not in-

---

3. See Clark H. Pinnock and Robert C. Brow, *Unbounded Love: A Good News Theology for the Twenty-first Century* (Downers Grove, Ill.: InterVarsity Press, 1994).

volve propitiation of the wrath of God, but only a change in human beings from alienation to love of God.

Assurance

Because of the emphasis on libertarian freedom in open theism, it is impossible to imagine how believers could be assured of their salvation. Since God has no control of our freedom, he has no right to promise that believers will persevere. And if he did make such a promise, he would be powerless to keep it.

Heaven and Hell

In open theism, it is not clear how even the saints in heaven can be assured of their salvation. For if they have libertarian free will, what is to prevent them from falling again? And if God takes from them the gift of free will, how can it have the value that open theists attribute to it?

In any case, many open theists seem to be gravitating toward views of eternal destiny that are inconsistent with traditional theology. Pinnock, for example, attempts "to interpret the nature of hell as the destruction rather than the endless torture of the wicked," a "conditional" view of the eternal state.[4] This view is perhaps part of the motivation behind the open-theist emphasis on love as the primary attribute of God (see chap. 4).

Guidance

As Bruce Ware stresses, there are grave problems in the implications of open theism for the doctrine of guidance. The

4. Clark H. Pinnock, "The Conditional View," in *Four Views on Hell,* ed. William Crockett (Grand Rapids: Zondervan, 1992), 137.

open theists argue that God can be wrong, and therefore that he sometimes gives bad advice. Christians have always regarded God as the paradigm of wisdom, one whose guidance is always reliable. But open theism leads us to question this fundamental proposition.[5] Roger Nicole points out the many occasions on which, according to open theism, God took risks and his plans failed: God made the angels, and many rebelled; he made Adam and Eve, and they turned against him; he repented of creation and had to destroy most of the human race; he hoped for better things from Noah's family, but those hopes were in vain, etc., etc. Nicole observes that, on this view,

> it is not God's plan but the lack of a plan that is the cause of the monumental problem of evil. I would not entrust my money to an earthly gambler with this kind of record! In fact I don't trust any gambler![6]

5. See Bruce A. Ware, *God's Lesser Glory* (Wheaton, Ill.: Crossway Books, 2000), 143–60.
6. Roger Nicole, "A Response to Gregory A. Boyd's *God of the Possible*," 24.

Conclusion

Open theism has provided a valuable service to us traditional theologians, for it has forced us to think harder about some important issues: God's love, his sovereign rule, human freedom, God's relationship to time and change, his suffering, and his knowledge. This encounter has led me to affirm, more strongly than before, God's exhaustive knowledge and his control of the world.

But it has also led me to rethink some other matters. I have concluded that there is indeed more "give-and-take" between God and his creatures than traditional theology has generally acknowledged. But I account for that mutual responsiveness, not by denying God's exhaustive sovereignty and knowledge, as in open theism, but by giving more emphasis to his temporal omnipresence. God stands above time and rules the world with absolute and infinite power and knowledge. But he also enters time and interacts personally with his creatures. His eternal plan includes and determines this personal interaction.

If traditional theology would put more emphasis (as Scripture certainly does) on the temporal interaction between God and the world, it would become less abstract, more practical, and more conducive to piety and obedience. And, rather than compromising God's sovereignty, it would present the workings of that sovereignty in richer detail, motivating us to be in even greater awe of the wisdom of God's ways in the world. It would also show us something of the importance of our own decisions. We have a role in accomplishing God's infinitely wise, eternal purposes!

I am grateful, therefore, to the open theists for the give-and-take with them that has enriched my thinking about God. But I am also deeply saddened by the course that their thinking has taken. They have denied God's sovereign lordship over his creation. They have denied his rule over time and his unchangeable eternal purpose. They have denied his exhaustive knowledge of the future. All for what? They have done all this to make their theology consistent with libertarian freedom—an incoherent, unbiblical speculation that denies divine sovereignty and destroys what it purports to establish, namely, human responsibility before God.

The gospel of grace is nothing if it is not good news about God's sovereign purpose. God's good news assures us that while we were yet sinners, Christ died for us (Rom. 5:8). God did not wait for man to assist him: he saw that no one could save himself, so he himself put on the armor of salvation (Isa. 59:9–21). Since he himself is the author of salvation, he guarantees that nothing will separate us from the love of Christ (Rom. 8:39). He accomplishes redemption in history, and he creates the response of faith in our hearts. He opens our hearts to respond to his message (Acts 16:14), so that all whom he has appointed to eternal life come to faith (Acts 13:48). At no point do we make the first move.

A gospel of grace is a gospel of divine sovereignty. That message may be distasteful to modern people, but it is the word of God, and without it we have no hope. Free will leaves us in despair. Only sovereign grace can bring salvation, faith, and hope.

Bibliography

Advocates of Open Theism

Basinger, David. *The Case for Freewill Theism: A Philosophical Assessment.* Downers Grove, Ill.: InterVarsity Press, 1996.

Basinger, David, and Randall Basinger. *Predestination and Free Will.* Downers Grove, Ill.: InterVarsity Press, 1986.

Boer, Harry R. *An Ember Still Glowing.* Grand Rapids: Eerdmans, 1990.

Boyd, Gregory A. *God at War: The Bible and Spiritual Conflict.* Downers Grove, Ill.: InterVarsity Press, 1997.

———. *God of the Possible.* Grand Rapids: Baker, 2000.

———. *Letters from a Skeptic.* Wheaton, Ill.: Victor Books, 1994.

———. *The Myth of the Blueprint.* Downers Grove, Ill.: InterVarsity Press, forthcoming.

———. *Satan and the Problem of Evil.* Downers Grove, Ill.: InterVarsity Press, forthcoming.

———. *Trinity and Process.* New York: Peter Lang, 1996.

Cobb, John B., and Clark H. Pinnock, eds. *Searching for an Adequate God: A Dialogue Between Process and Free Will Theists.* Grand Rapids: Eerdmans, 2000.

Davis, Stephen T. *Logic and the Nature of God.* Grand Rapids: Eerdmans, 1983.

Elseth, H. Roy. *Did God Know? A Study of the Nature of God.* St. Paul: Calvary United Church, 1977.

Geach, Peter. *Providence and Evil.* Cambridge: Cambridge University Press, 1977.

Hasker, William. "Foreknowledge and Necessity." In *Faith and Philosophy* 2, no. 2 (April 1985): 121–57.

———. *God, Time, and Knowledge.* Ithaca, N.Y.: Cornell University Press, 1989.

———. "The Openness of God," *Christian Scholar's Review* 28, no. 1 (fall 1998): 111–39.

Johnson, Elizabeth A. *She Who Is.* New York: Crossroad, 1992.

Kitamori, Kayoh. *Theology of the Pain of God.* Richmond: John Knox Press, 1965.

LaCugna, Catherine Mowry. *God for Us.* New York: Crossroad, 1992.

Lucas, J. R. *The Freedom of the Will.* Oxford: Oxford University Press, 1970.

———. *The Future: An Essay on God, Temporality, and Truth.* London: Blackwell, 1989.

McCabe, L. D. *Divine Nescience of Future Contingencies a Necessity.* New York: Phillips and Hunt, 1882.

———. *The Foreknowledge of God.* Cincinnati: Cranston and Stowe, 1887.

Moltmann, Jürgen. *The Crucified God.* London: SCM Press, 1974.

Olson, Gordon. *The Foreknowledge of God.* Arlington Heights, Ill.: Bible Research Corporation, 1941.

———. *The Omniscience of the Godhead.* Arlington Heights, Ill.: Bible Research Corporation, 1972.

Pinnock, Clark H. "Between Classical and Process Theism." In *Process Theology,* ed. Ronald H. Nash. Grand Rapids: Baker, 1987.

———. "God Limits His Knowledge." In *Predestination and Free Will,* ed. David Basinger and Randall Basinger. Downers Grove, Ill.: InterVarsity Press, 1986.

———. *A Wideness in God's Mercy.* Grand Rapids: Zondervan, 1992.

Pinnock, Clark H., and Robert C. Brow. *Unbounded Love: A Good News Theology for the Twenty-first Century.* Downers Grove, Ill.: InterVarsity Press, 1994.

Pinnock, Clark H., Richard Rice, John Sanders, William Hasker, and David Basinger. *The Openness of God.* Downers Grove, Ill.: InterVarsity Press, 1994.

Pinnock, Clark H., ed. *The Grace of God and the Will of Man.* Grand Rapids: Zondervan, 1989. Some articles written from a traditional Arminian perspective, others leaning toward open theism.

Rice, Richard. *God's Foreknowledge and Man's Free Will.* Minneapolis: Bethany House, 1985.

Sanders, John. "God as Personal." In *The Grace of God and the Will of Man,* ed. Clark H. Pinnock. Grand Rapids: Zondervan, 1989.

———. *The God Who Risks.* Downers Grove, Ill.: InterVarsity Press, 1998.

———. *No Other Name: An Investigation into the Destiny of the Unevangelized.* Grand Rapids: Eerdmans, 1992.

Swinburne, Richard. *The Coherence of Theism.* Oxford: Clarendon Press, 1977. Philosophical treatment.

Wolterstorff, Nicholas. "God Everlasting." In *God and the Good,* ed. Clifton Orlebeke and Lewis Smedes, 181–203. Grand Rapids: Eerdmans, 1975. On God's relationship to time.

Critiques

Beckwith, Francis, "God Knows?" Review of Gregory Boyd's *God of the Possible. Christian Scholar's Review* 22, no. 4 (2000): 54–55.

Caneday, A. B. "The Implausible God of Open Theism: A Response to Gregory A. Boyd's *God of the Possible.*" *Journal of Biblical Apologetics* 1 (fall 200): 66–87.

———. "Putting God at Risk: A Critique of John Sanders's View of Providence." *Trinity Journal,* n.s., 20 (1999): 131–63.

Erickson, Millard J. *God the Father Almighty.* Grand Rapids: Baker, 1998.

Fackre, Gabriel. "An Evangelical Megashift? The Promise and Peril of an 'Open' View of God." *Christian Century,* May 3, 1995, 484–87.

Frame, John M. *The Doctrine of God.* Phillipsburg, N.J.: P&R Publishing, forthcoming.

Helm, Paul. *Eternal God.* Oxford: Clarendon Press, 1988. Defends the timeless eternity of God philosophically.

———. "God and Spacelessness." *Philosophy* 55 (1980): 211–21.

———. *The Providence of God.* Leicester: InterVarsity Press, 1993. Defends a "no risk" view of providence.

Helseth, Paul Kjoss, "On Divine Ambivalence: Open Theism and the Problem of Particular Evils." *Journal of the Evangelical Theological Society.* Forthcoming.

Mohler, R. Albert. "Does God Give Bad Advice?" *World* 15, no. 24 (June 1, 2000): 23.

Nicole, Roger. "A Review Article: God of the Possible?" *Reformation and Revival* 10, no. 1 (winter, 2001), 167–94.

———. "Review of *The Openness of God.*" *Founders Journal* (fall, 1995).

Piper, John, with Justin Taylor (appendix by Millard Erickson). *Resolution on the Foreknowledge of God: Reasons and Rationale* (Minneapolis: Bethlehem Baptist Church, 2000).

Roy, Steven C., "How Much Does God Foreknow?" Ph.D. diss., Trinity International University.

Schreiner, Thomas R., and Bruce A. Ware. *The Grace of God, the Bondage of the Will.* Grand Rapids: Baker, 1995. Calvinistic views of divine sovereignty and man's bondage under sin. Some references to open theists, but mostly positive expositions of Reformed perspectives.

Schreiner, Thomas R., and Bruce A. Ware, eds. *Still Sovereign: Contemporary Perspectives on Election, Foreknowledge, and Grace* (Grand Rapids: Baker, 2000).

Strimple, Robert B. "What Does God Know?" In *The Coming Evangelical Crisis,* ed. John H. Armstrong. Chicago: Moody Press, 1996.

Veith, Gene. "The Opening of the American God." *World* 15, no. 24 (June 1, 2000): 25–26.

Ware, Bruce A. "Despair Amidst Suffering and Pain: A Practical Outworking of Open Theism's Diminished View of God." *The Southern Baptist Journal of Theology* 4, no. 2 (summer 2000), 56–57.

———. "An Evangelical Reformulation of the Doctrine of the Immutability of God," *Journal of the Evangelical Theological Society* 29, no. 4 (1986), 431–46.

———. *God's Lesser Glory: The Diminished God of Open Theism.* Wheaton, Ill.: Crossway Books, 2000.

———. Review of *The Case for Free Will Theism. Journal of the Evangelical Theological Society* 43:1 (March 2000), 165–68.

Williams, Stephen N. "What God Doesn't Know: Were the Biblical Prophecies Mere Probabilities?" Review of *The God Who Risks,* by John Sanders. *Books and Culture,* November-December, 1999, 16–18.

Wilson, Douglas. *Knowledge, Foreknowledge, and the Gospel.* Moscow, Ida.: Canon Press, 1997.

Wilson, Douglas, ed. *Bound Only Once: The Openness of God as a Failure of Imagination, Nerve, and Reason.* Forthcoming from Canon Press.

Wright, R. K. McGregor. *No Place for Sovereignty: What's Wrong with Freewill Theism.* Downers Grove, Ill.: InterVarsity Press, 1996.

See also Reformed confessions and systematic theologies on these subjects: the divine attributes (especially knowledge, eternity, and unchangeability), God's decrees, providence, election, effectual calling, and regeneration.

Mixed Affirmation and Criticism

Craig, William Lane, Gregory Boyd, Paul Helm, and David Hunt. *Divine Foreknowledge: Four Views.* Downers Grove, Ill.: InterVarsity Press, forthcoming.

"God vs. God." *Christianity Today,* February 7, 2000, 34–35.

"Has God Been Held Hostage by Philosophy?" *Christianity Today,* January 9, 1995, 30–34.

Olson, Roger E. "Postconservative Evangelicals Greet the Postmodern Age." *Christian Century,* May 3, 1995, 480–81.

Resources

These works deal with various issues of the controversy, but do not specifically address open theism.

Augustine. *The City of God.* Various editions.

———. *Confessions.* Various editions.

Bavinck, Herman. *The Doctrine of God.* Grand Rapids: Baker, 1951.

Buswell, J. Oliver. *A Systematic Theology of the Christian Religion.* Grand Rapids: Zondervan, 1962. In the Presbyterian tradition, but argues for the temporality of God and tends toward libertarianism.

Calvin, John. *Concerning the Eternal Predestination of God.* London: James Clark, 1951.

———. *Institutes of the Christian Religion.* Translated by Ford Lewis Battles. Edited by John T. McNeill. The Library of Christian Classics. 2 vols. Philadelphia: Westminster Press, 1960.

Campbell, C. A. "The Psychology of Effort of Will." *Proceedings of the Aristotelian Society* 40 (1939–40): 49–74. Secular defense of libertarianism.

Carson, D. A. *Divine Sovereignty and Human Responsibility.* Atlanta: John Knox Press, 1981. Calvinistic position.

Chisholm, Robert B. "Does God 'Change His Mind'?" Address delivered at the Evangelical Theological Society Annual Meeting, 1994.

Cobb, John B., Jr., and David Ray Griffin. *Process Theology: An Introductory Exposition.* Philadelphia: Westminster Press, 1976.

Cottrell, Jack. *What the Bible Says About God the Ruler.* Joplin, Mo.: College Press, 1984. An able statement of a traditional Arminian position.

Creel, Richard E. *Divine Impassibility.* Cambridge: Cambridge University Press, 1986. Defends some aspects of the traditional view.

Edwards, Jonathan. *Freedom of the Will.* Reprint, New Haven: Yale University Press, 1973. Classic Calvinist critique of libertarianism.

Farley, Benjamin W. *The Providence of God in Reformed Perspective.* Grand Rapids: Baker, 1988. In the Reformed tradition, but verges on libertarianism. See my review in *Westminster Theological Journal* 51 (1989): 397–400.

Frame, John M. *Apologetics to the Glory of God.* Phillipsburg, N.J.: P&R Publishing, 1994.

———. *Cornelius Van Til.* Phillipsburg, N.J.: P&R Publishing, 1995.

———. *The Doctrine of the Knowledge of God.* Phillipsburg, N.J.: Presbyterian and Reformed, 1987.

Fretheim, Terence E. *The Suffering of God.* Philadelphia: Fortress, 1984. Gives some exegetical support to open theism.

Gruenler, Royce Gordon. *The Inexhaustible God.* Grand Rapids: Baker, 1983. Reformed evangelical gives his reasons for rejecting process theology.

Hobart, R. E. "Free Will as Involving Determinism and as Inconceivable Without It." *Mind* 43 (1934): 7. A secular critique of libertarianism.

Hodge, Charles. *Systematic Theology.* 3 vols. Reprint, Grand Rapids: Eerdmans, n.d.

Lindström, Fredrik. *God and the Origin of Evil.* Lund: CWK Gleerup, 1983.

Luther, Martin. *The Bondage of the Will.* London: J. Clarke, 1957.

Nash, Ronald H., ed. *Process Theology.* Grand Rapids: Baker. 1987.

Pratt, Richard. "Historical Contingencies and Biblical Predictions." www.thirdmill.org

Weinandy, Thomas G. *Does God Suffer?* Notre Dame, Ind.: University of Notre Dame Press, 2000. Answers no.

Web Sites

The Edgren Foundation
http://www.edgren.org
Open View Theism Index (Christus Victor Ministries)
http:www.gregboyd.org/gbfront/index.asp?PageID=257
Open Theism Webpage
http://www.opentheism.org

Index of Scripture

Genesis
1—90
1:1—181
1:3—82n
1:5—154, 177
1:8—177
1:10—177
1:14—154
1:28—18
2:7—59
3—30
3:9—194
3:14–19—85
4:1—62
4:25—62
6:3—122
6:5—161, 163
6:6—180
8:1—195
8:22—58
9:14–16—195n
9:15–16—195
9:26–27—200
11:5—194
12:1–3—97
15:5—202
15:13–16—200
17:7—158

18:13–14—62
18:14—114
18:16–33—165, 166
18:20–21—194
18:25—59
21:13—125
22—197, 206
22:12—47–48, 193, 194
22:14—194n
25:21—62
27:27–29—200
27:39–40—200
29:31–30:2—62
30:17—62
30:23–24—62
33:19—101
35:5—60
41:16—60
41:28—60
41:32—58, 60
45:5–8—60, 64
49:1–28—200
50:20—60, 110, 127

Exodus
3:13–15—54
3:19—69

3:21–22—65
4:11—140
4:21—69
6:5—195
6:7—54
7:3—69
7:5—54
7:13—69
7:17—54
8:15—69
8:22—54
9:12—69
9:13–26—58
9:16—65, 101
10:1—69
10:2—54
10:20—69
10:27—69
11:10—69
12:36—65
14:4—54, 65, 69
14:8—69
14:17–18—69n
14:18—54
20:1–3—50
20:5—50
21:12–13—63
21:12–14—124

21:13—58
23:27—63
32—197
32:9–10—163
32:9–14—165, 166
32:12—163
32:14—163
33:19—51, 117
34—164
34:6–7—50, 164, 165
34:14—50
34:24—66

Leviticus
18:21—195
20:8—82
26:12—158

Numbers
23–24—200
23:19—37n, 162, 163
35:10–34—124

Deuteronomy
2:25—60
2:30—70
3:22—60
4:6—81n
6:4–9—50
7:8—53
10:22—62
13:3—193, 194
18:10—196
18:21–22—67n, 115, 167–68
18:22—199
28—169
29:4—74n, 81
30:6—81
30:19—133
31:16–21—197
31:32—197
32:1–43—200
32:39—118, 140, 162
32:40—152
33:1–29—200

Joshua
11:18–20—70

21:44–45—60
24:11—60

Judges
7:22—66
9:23—70n
9:53—58
14:4—71

Ruth
1:13—63
4:13—62

1 Samuel
2:6–7—63, 140
2:25—70
10:1–7—168, 201
10:9—65n
15:29—162, 163
15:35—163
16:4—70
17:47—60

2 Samuel
17:14—72
24—71

1 Kings
3:12—65n
8:5–8—82
8:58–61—127
12:15—72
13:1–3—62n
13:1–4—201
22:20–23—70
22:34—58

2 Kings
8:12—201
19:5–7—70n

1 Chronicles
21:15—165n
29:14–19—82

2 Chronicles
7:11—195
20:6—16n

20:15—60
25:20—70, 72

Ezra
1:1—61
6:22—66

Nehemiah
7:5—195

Job
1–2—138n
1:21—139
23:1–7—138
31:35–37—138
38–40—58
38–42—68
38:3—138
41:11—87
42:2—114, 139
42:11—139

Psalms
1:6—77
5:4—111
9:18—195
13:1—195
22:18—66
33:10–11—59
33:11—118, 152, 162, 173
33:15—65
37:23—63
41:9—72
44:21—194
45:6–12—59
47:1–9—59
50:10–11—202
51:18—111
56:8—202
65:4—117
65:9–11—58
71:22—50
73:11—35
78:41—50
89:18—50
89:34–37—174
90:4—155
93:2—152

95:3—59
95:7-8—69
102:24—152
102:25-27—162, 172
102:27—152
103:8—53
103:21—111
104:10-30—58
104:24—202
105:24—69
106:41-45—165n
107:23-32—58
110:4—162, 169
111:10—81n
113:9—62
115:3—111, 118, 130
127:3-5—62
135:5-7—58
135:6—106, 118
136—21
139:1—194
139:4-6—62
139:17-18—202
139:23-24—194
145:13—152
145:15-16—51
146:10—152
147:4—202
147:8-9—58
147:15-18—58

Proverbs
1:7—81n
9:10—81n
15:33—81n
16:1—65
16:4—74
16:4-5—127
16:5—74n
16:9—65, 115
16:33—58
19:21—65, 115
21:1—65
21:30—115
21:31—60

Ecclesiastes
7:13-14—140

Isaiah
1:4—50
1:9—97
5:1-7—197
6—72
6:3—51
6:7—51
6:9-10—81
6:10—70
7:5—51
8:22—51
10:5-11—71
10:5-12—60
10:5-15—127
10:6—71
10:20-22—97
11:11—97
11:16—97
14:24—169
14:24-25—60
14:24-27—114
14:26-27—60
17—51
29:10—73
29:16—116
30:18—112
31:2—115
33:6—81n
37:26—60
38:1-5—166
40-55—90
40-66—90
40:13—87
40:21—153, 175
40:26—202
40:28—202
41:2—177
41:4—153, 175, 177
41:21-23—199
41:21-29—35
41:22—35
41:26—153
42:6—90
42:7—90
42:9—199
43:9-12—199
43:12—175
43:12-13—118

43:13—162
44:7—199
44:28—61, 64
44:28-45:13—201
45:1-6—91
45:1-13—61
45:5-7—140
45:6—91
45:7—90-92
45:8—90-91
45:9—116
45:9-11—90-91
45:10-11—90
45:11—91
45:12—90-91
45:18—90
45:23—169
46:10—111, 115,
  153, 175, 199
47:5—90
48:3-7—199
49:6—90
49:9—90
53:3-4—189
53:11—90
54:8—53
54:9—169
54:10—174
55:11—115
59:9-21—212
62:8—169
63:9—19, 53, 184,
  188
63:17—71
64:7—71
64:8—116
65:2—112
65:12—117

Jeremiah
1:5—62, 201
3—196
3:6-7—196, 197n
3:7—196n
3:14-25—197
3:19-20—196
4:28—162, 169
7:15—168

7:16—168
7:23—158
7:31—195
10:23—63n
11:4—158
15:6—162
17:9—68
18—37n, 86n, 167
18:1–4—167
18:1–10—116
18:5–10—115n,
    165–67, 169
19:5—195
20:16—162
23:20—114, 169
23:27—114
23:39—195
24:7—81
26:3—166, 194, 196,
    197
26:13—166
26:19—166
29:10–14—127
29:11–14—60
30:4–24—61
30:22—158
30:24—169
31:3—53
31:31–34—81
32:35—194, 195
32:39–40—82
33:22—202
36:3—196, 197
36:7—196
37:6–11—201
42:10—166
44:26—169
49:13—169
49:20—111
50:45—111
51:14—169

Lamentations
3:31–36—112
3:37–38—84, 87, 140

Ezekiel
5:11—169

11:19—81
11:20—117
12:3—194, 196
14:16—169
14:18—169
14:20—169
18:23—112
18:25—139n
20:3—169
20:31—169
20:33—169
24:14—162, 169
33:11—22, 112, 180
33:27—169
35:6—169
35:11—169
36:26—81
36:26–27—117
36:28—158
38:16—71

Daniel
1:9—66
2:21—61, 95
2:38–40—94
4:17—111
4:34–35—61, 95
4:35—106, 115
7:1–28—67n
9:20–27—201

Hosea
11:1—67n
11:7–8—112
13:4—77

Joel
2:13–14—164, 165

Amos
1:3—169
1:6—169
1:9—169
1:13—169
2:1—169
2:4—169
2:6—169
3:2—77

3:6—140
4:2—169
4:7—58
6:8—169
7:1–6—164, 166,
    167, 176
8:7—169

Jonah
2:9—74
3:4—165, 167
3:9—168
3:10—37n, 161
4:1–2—165
4:2—168

Micah
7:19–20—173

Haggai
1:14—82

Zechariah
1:6—115
4:6—60
8:6—114
8:14—169
8:14–15—162
12:10—79

Malachi
3:6—154, 162, 173

Matthew
1:20–23—66
1:22—61
2:14–15—66, 67n
2:15—61
2:22–23—66
3:3—61
4:12–16—66–67
4:14—61
5:45—58
6:9—16n
6:26–27—58
6:28–30—58
7:15–20—127, 131

7:21—111
10:29—58
10:30—58, 202
10:31—59
11:25–26—110, 116
11:25–27—81
12:33–35—131
12:50—111
13:14–15—72
16:21—67
17:21—133
19:4—153
19:26—114
20:1–16—139n
20:16—80
21:1–5—67
22:14—80
23:37–39—117
24:6—67
24:22—99
24:24—99
24:31—99
24:36—61
25:12—77
26:34—201
26:55–56—67
27:46—188
28:18–20—186

Mark
8:31—67
9:11—67
13:7—67
13:10—67
13:14—67
13:20–22—99
13:32—156
14:49—67

Luke
1:37—114
6:43–45—127
6:45—65, 131
7:30—117
9:22—67
12:13–21—63n
12:47–48—125
17:25—67

18:7—99
19:41—182
22:22—61, 64, 73, 127
24:26—67

John
1:1—153
1:12—75
1:12–13—127
1:13—78n, 80n
3:3—80
3:5–6—80
3:8—80
3:15–16—75
3:16—53
3:34–35—50
3:36—76
4:34—111
5:21—117
6:29—75
6:37—78, 117, 127
6:40—75
6:44—78
6:64—121
6:65—78
6:66–67—97
6:70—117n
6:70–71—97, 121
7:17—111
8:34–36—131
10:14—77
10:16—78n
10:26—79n
10:28—79n
10:28–29—56
10:38—187
11:26—7
11:35—182
11:51—78n
12:20–22—78n
12:32—78n
12:40—72
13:18—72
13:18–19—121
13:48—79
14:10–11—187
14:15—76

14:20—187
14:21—76
14:23—76
15:5—82, 83
15:16—76n, 78
15:25—72
17—79n
17:2—79n
17:6—79n
17:6–8—79n
17:12—121
17:21—187
18:10—78n
19:24—66
19:31–37—66
20:28—54
21:6—78n
21:11—78n

Acts
1:7—156
2:23—73, 111, 127
2:23–24—61, 64, 185
2:36—54
3:18—61, 64
4:27–28—61, 64, 127
4:28—73
5:31—80
5:39—102
7:26—59
7:51—117
11:18—80
11:21—79
11:23—79
13:27—61, 64, 73
13:27–29—67
13:48—75, 79, 99, 212
13:48–14:1—127
14:17—58
16:14—212
16:14–15—78
16:19—78n
17:25—179
17:26—156
18:10—79n
18:27—79
21:30—78n

Romans

1—80
1:6–7—80
1:16—176
1:19–20—73
1:21–25—73
1:24–27—122
1:24–28—73
1:24–32—70n
3:3–8—139n
3:21–4:25—99n
3:31—139n
5:8—53, 212
6:1–2—139n
6:4—82
6:15—139
6:15–23—131
7:7—139n
7:18—82
8:6–8—82
8:15—78
8:18—85
8:21—85
8:22—85
8:28—84
8:28–39—68, 98
8:29—76, 77, 77n
8:29–30—117
8:30—80, 98
8:31–39—180
8:32—53
8:33—87n
8:33–34—98
8:35—56
8:35–39—98
8:38–39—85
8:39—212
9—86n, 99, 99n, 100, 116
9–10—127
9–11—73, 86, 96, 99, 101n
9:1–13—97
9:2—99
9:6—100
9:6–9—100
9:10–13—100
9:11—87n, 100

9:12—100
9:13—100
9:14—101
9:15—101
9:15–18—96
9:16—101
9:16–18—100
9:17—65, 69, 101
9:17–24—68
9:18—69, 101, 117
9:18–19—111
9:19—86n
9:19–21—86n, 101, 116, 138
9:19–24—116
9:21–24—86
9:22—102
9:22–26—73
9:30–32—95, 96
9:30–10:21—102
9:33–36—87
10:9—54
11:1–10—102
11:2—77
11:5—102
11:7–8—73
11:7–10—102
11:11–16—73
11:11–32—100
11:22—96
11:25–32—73
11:28—87n
11:29—80
11:33—87, 111
11:33–36—87, 180, 183n, 202
11:36—87, 93
12:2—111
12:3—79
12:3–6—63
12:3–8—83
15:4—175

1 Corinthians

1:2—80
1:9—80
1:18—185
1:21—186

1:23–24—185
1:24—80, 186
1:25—185
1:26—80
1:27–28—99
1:29—83
2:4–5—81
2:5—79
2:7—81
2:12–16—81
4:7—63, 83
8:3—77
12:1–11—83
12:3—54
12:4–6—63
13—50

2 Corinthians

2:15–16—72
3:5—83
3:17—131
4:6—82
4:7—83
5:17—82
6:2—158
6:16—158
10:17—83
11:11—202
12:2–3—202
12:9—187
12:9–10—187

Galatians

4:4—61, 155

Ephesians

1:3–14—98
1:4—62, 86, 98, 99
1:4–5—77, 116
1:4–6—75
1:5—86
1:5–14—98
1:7–10—99
1:9—116
1:11—85–86, 87, 93, 94, 111, 130, 202
1:12—99
1:13–14—99

1:15–23—99
1:17–19—81
2:1—74, 80, 82
2:3—74
2:4–10—75
2:9—83
2:10—82, 99
4:1–13—83
4:30—19, 117, 180
5:17—111
5:25–27—82
6:6—111
6:10–20—186
6:23—79

Philippians
1:6—82
1:29—79
2:1–11——50
2:11—54
2:12–13—127
2:13—82
4:13—18

Colossians
1:9—81
1:10–12—82
3:1–3—127
3:12—99
4:3—18

1 Thessalonians
1:4—75
1:4–5—79, 99
1:5—81
4:3—111
5:9—75, 118
5:12—77
5:18—111
5:19—117

2 Thessalonians
2:11–12—70n

2:13—99
2:13–14—75, 80
2:14—81

2 Timothy
1:9—75, 99
2:10—99
2:25—80
3:16–17—175

Titus
1:1—99
3:4–7—82

Hebrews
1:5–8—173
1:10—153
1:10–12—172
2:17—184
3:1—80
3:2—80
4:2—117
4:13—202
6:4–6—97
6:17–20—175
7:21—162
8:13—175
10:26–31—97
12:25—117
13:8—172, 174
13:21—111

James
1:5—81
1:14—133
1:17—37n, 162, 172
1:18—111
2:5—99
2:6—78n
4:13–16—63

1 Peter
1:2—76
1:3–7—158

1:20—77
2:6–8—72
2:13–3:22—186
4:2—111
4:12–19—186

2 Peter
1:10—80
3:8—155
3:9—112

1 John
1:5—50, 51
1:8–10—82
2:19—97
2:20–21—81
2:27—81
2:29—80n
3:9—80n
3:16—50
3:20—202
4:7—80n
4:8—50, 51
4:8–10—53
4:10—50
4:15–16—53
4:16—50
4:24—50
5:1—80n
5:4—80n
5:18—80n
5:20—81

Revelation
3:7—18, 118
3:8—18
4:11—111
10:6—152n
15:3–4—141
15:34—68
17:17—74
21:14—141
21:34—158

Index of Names and Subjects

ability, and moral guilt, 124–25
Abraham, 47, 97, 193, 200
Absalom, 71–72
"actual infinite," 147, 151
Adam, 131
Alexander, Samuel, 38
ambiguous language, 19–21
Amos, 164, 167, 176
Anaximander, 29
Anaximenes, 29
angels, 105, 209
Anselm, 144, 182
antecedent will, 108, 110
anthropomorphism, 12, 47–48,
    176–77, 181, 198
antinomies, 42–43
Apostles' Creed, 192n
application, 41
Aquinas, Thomas, 49, 144, 150
Arian controversy, 143
Aristotle, 28–29, 32, 181
Arminianism, 22, 39–40, 76, 78,
    108, 123, 128–29, 135,
    192n
Arminius, Jacob, 28, 33
aseity, 179–80, 182
assurance, 203
Assyrians, 71

atemporal consciousness, 155
atonement, 207
Augustine, 27n, 122, 144–45,
    152n, 157
autonomy, 30, 35, 113

Balaam, 200
Barr, James, 145, 149, 151–53
Barth, Karl, 50, 53
Bavinck, Herman, 49–50, 171
Being, 49
Bergson, Henri, 37
Berkhof, Henrikus, 38
Bertocci, Peter, 37
Bible, 27, 41
    contradictions in, 42–45
    on God as unchanging, 162
    on God's ignorance, 193–98
    on God's knowledge of future,
        198–203
    on God's relenting, 163–66
    inerrancy, 207
    inspiration, 84, 205–6
    and modern culture, 36
    on time, 151–59
blessing, 169–70
Boethius, 144–45, 150, 157
Bohm, David, 150n

Boston Personalism, 37, 146n
Bowne, Borden P., 37
Boyd, Gregory A., 37n, 77n, 86n,
    87, 139n, 191–92n, 195n
    on divine sovereignty, 95–96
    on election, 99n
    on the future, 94
    on guidance, 206
    on libertarian freedom,
      121–22, 125
    on Peter's denial of Christ, 201–2
Bradley, F. H., 37
Brightman, Edgar S., 37, 146n
Brunner, Emil, 38, 50, 53
Buber, Martin, 50
Buswell, James Oliver, 145, 148n

calling, 80
calmness, 181
Calvin, John, 35, 92, 122, 144n,
    166
Calvinism, 22, 28, 30, 106–7,
    119n, 128
Cambridge changes, 170–72
Carson, D. A., 181–82
causation, 29, 124, 130
chance, 20, 28n, 30, 37, 93
change, 21, 154, 170–72
character, 126, 127, 128, 131
choice, 75–76, 78, 120, 125
church fathers, 27
circumcessio, 187
civil courts, 126
Clark, Gordon H., 50n
Clarke, Adam, 37n
Clarke, W. Norris, 150
Cobb, John, 38
coercion, 29
compatibilist freedom, 123n, 131–34
conditional prophecy, 169, 199
confidence, 85
consequent will, 108, 110
consummation, 86, 114, 158
contingencies, 16
contradictions, in Bible, 42–45
Council of Chalcedon, 187
covenant, 77, 97, 99n, 100, 158–59,
    169, 173–75, 195, 197

creation, 87, 112, 147–48,
    153–54, 177
Creator-creature distinction, 172
cross of Jesus, 114, 140, 185–86
Cullmann, Oscar, 145, 149,
    151–53, 157
culture, 25–26
curse, 169–70, 195
Cyrus, 61, 91–92, 201

Daniel, 94–95
David, 71–72
decretive will, 22n, 44,
    109–12, 167, 168–69,
    173, 176, 178
Demiurge, 28–29, 32
desires, prioritizing of, 107
determinism, 30, 95, 127n, 132
Dorner, I. A., 50
dualism, 93
Duns Scotus, 50, 144

effectual calling, 80
Egypt, 68–69
Einstein, Albert, 150
election, 75–76, 77, 86, 96–102
    corporate, 97, 98, 99
    eternal, 97–98, 100
    historical, 97–98, 100
    individual, 99
emotions, 180–85
empires, rise and fall, 94–95
Epicurus, 28
Esau, 100
eternal life, 152
eternal punishment, 52n
eternity, 143–45, 151–53
evangelicalism, 39
evil, 140
exegesis, 45, 47–48, 124

faith, 74, 76n, 79, 95–96
fall, 30, 131
false prophet, 168
feminist theology, 179n
Fiske, John, 37
foreknowledge, 76–78
    entails foreordination, 40

without foreordination,
128–29
foreordination, 22, 24, 33
forms, 28–29
freedom, 20
in modern culture, 25–26
from sin, 131
freewill theism, 119, 206
See also open theism
fulfillment of prophecy, 67n

Gamaliel, 103
genetic fallacy, 26n
Gentiles, hardening of, 73
Gnosticism, 37n
God
as aloof monarch, 15, 17, 32
aseity, 150, 179–80, 182,
189
attributes, 49–52, 172
as caring parent, 16
as closed, 18
compassion, 184
consciousness, 155
control of history, 59–61
control of human lives, 61–63
control of nature, 58, 92–93
covenant faithfulness, 173–75
decrees, 84, 113–18
dynamic relation to, 20–21
emotions, 180–85
essence, 51–52
eternity, 143–45
experiences frustration, 105,
191
extraordinary acts, 102–3
fairness, 86
as finite, 37
foreknowledge, 32–33, 35, 39,
65n, 136, 191, 198
foreordination, 22, 24, 33, 65,
140
giving bad advice, 209
as grieved, 19, 163, 180, 184,
188
immanence, 147, 159, 176–77,
183
impassibility, 31, 179

incomprehensibility, 86
incorporeality, 182
knowledge as unchanging, 173
lordship, 51, 54, 156–57,
158–59
love, 21, 49–50, 52, 53–56
omnipotence, 113, 173
omnipresence, 198
omniscience, 150, 192
"paths," 111
pleasure, 115
relenting, 46, 115n, 163–66,
196
remembering and forgetting,
195
as risk-taker, 45–46, 105
sovereignty, 18, 51, 58, 87, 92,
93, 123, 130, 139–41, 159,
167, 178, 186, 198
and human responsibility,
95–96
limited, 130
over sin, 67–74
in salvation, 74–83
and space, 149
suffering, 187–89
and time, 143–59
transcendence, 138, 147, 153,
159, 176–78, 183, 188
two models, 15–17
unchangeability, 31, 115n,
150, 154, 161, 170–75,
182, 189
vulnerability, 17, 19, 38,
55–56, 179
weakness, 185–87
will, 23, 57n, 106–8
wisdom, 173
wrath, 52, 54
gospel, 75, 212
grace, 75, 83, 117–18, 171, 212
greater good defense, 140
Greek philosophy, 16n, 20, 26,
30, 31–32, 143, 149–50,
181–82
Griffin, David Ray, 38
guidance, 206, 208–9
Gunton, Colin, 38

Hannah, 63
hardening of one's heart, 69–71, 73
Hartshorne, Charles, 38
Hasker, William, 23, 120
heart, 65, 195
heaven, 125, 141, 208
Hegel, G., 50
Heisenberg's uncertainty principle, 33
hell, 208
Helm, Paul, 146, 148, 185
Heschel, A., 53
Hilary of Poitiers, 144n
historiography, 34n
history, 57, 59–61, 114, 176–78
Hobart, R. E., 127n
Hodge, Charles, 145
Holy Spirit, 81
human decision, 64–67
human responsibility, 95–96, 124, 126
Hume, David, 37

Idealism, 37
ideas, 28–29
ignorance, 154
imputed righteousness, 207
incarnation, 56, 182, 187–88
infinity, 151
intuition, 129–30
Irenaeus, 27n
irresistible grace, 117–18
Isaac, 100, 200
Isaiah, 70–71
Ishmael, 100
Israel, 97
    hardened hearts, 70–71
    idolatry, 196–97
    unbelief, 73, 100–102, 117n

Jacob, 100, 200
Jacobie, 50
James, William, 37
Jansenius, Cornelius, 50
Jeremiah, 62, 64
Jeroboam, 201
Jesus
    atonement, 85
    death, 73, 114, 140, 185–86, 187–90
    use of parables, 72
Job, 137n, 138–39
Joel, 164
Johnson, Elizabeth, 38
Jonah, 165–68
Joseph, 59–60, 64, 68–69
Josiah, 201
Judas, 117n, 121–22, 125, 200
judgment, 52, 169–70, 196
Jüngel, Eberhard, 38
Justin Martyr, 27n

Kant, Immanuel, 37
Kasper, W., 53
Kelly, Douglas F., 34n
knowledge of God, 81
Knudson, Albert C., 37

LaGugna, Catherine, 38
law of noncontradiction, 44
libertarian freedom, 20, 23–24, 27–31, 35, 108–9, 113, 119–31, 212
    and divine omniscience, 192–93
    as independence, 127
    and moral responsibility, 126
    and the problem of evil, 134, 141
    and temporality of God, 146, 156–57
    as ultimate presupposition, 42, 46
light, 90–91
Lindström, Fredrik, 89–90
literal interpretation, 48
logic, 42–45
Lotze, H., 50
love, as God's primary attribute, 49–50, 52–56, 208
Luther, Martin, 19n, 122, 144n
Lutheran theologians, 108
Lydia, 78

McGrath, Alister E., 19n, 34n
Marshall, I. Howard, 133n

means, and ends, 167
Melanchthon, 35
metaphors, 45
Mill, John Stuart, 37
mind, 195
miracles, 102, 103n
models, 45–46
modern culture, 25–26, 33, 36
modern theology, 26
Molinists, 122
Moltmann, Jürgen, 38, 50, 187
moral guilt, and ability, 124–25
moral influence theory of the
    atonement, 207
moral responsibility, 28n
Morey, Robert A., 37n
Moses, 200
motives, 126
Muller, Richard, 123n
Murray, John, 73
mysteries, 44, 137

Naomi, 63
natural world, 58
Nebuchadnezzar, 94–95
necessity, and human freedom, 67
Neoplatonism, 30, 37n, 181
new age, 158
newness, 26–27
Nicene Creed, 192n
Nicodemus, 80
Nicole, Roger, 37n, 105, 136n, 209
Nineveh, 165–68
Noah, 105, 200, 209

obedience, 166
Ogden, Schubert, 38
Olson, Roger, 26, 30
omniscience, 34
open theism
    as evangelical movement, 39
    on foreknowledge, 78
    resembles Greek philosophy,
        30, 31–32
    service to traditional theism, 211
openness, 17–18
Origen, 128
original sin, 207

panentheism, 32, 149
Pannenberg, Wolfhart, 38, 53, 171
pantheism, 32, 149
Parmenides, 143
passions, 182–83
Paul, 72–73, 83
Pelagian controversy, 122
personality, unity of, 127
perspectives, 52–53, 54
persuasion, 29
Peter, denial of Christ, 201–2
Pharaoh, 69–70, 100–102, 200
Philo, 27
Pinnock, Clark
    on evil, 135
    exegesis of the Bible, 42
    on freedom, 23, 122, 129
    on God's ignorance, 193–94
    on God's love, 55
    on God's power, 122
    on God's unchangeability,
        161
    on God's vulnerability, 179
    on Greek philosophy, 31–32
    on hell, 208
    on logic, 44
    on modern culture, 25–26
    on mystery, 137n
    on omniscience, 192
    and openness, 18
    and Socinianism, 34–45
    on time, 147
    two models of God, 15–17
Plato, 28–29, 32, 143
Platonism, 152, 181
Plotinus, 143
polytheism, 93
potter and clay analogy, 86, 116,
    167
Pratt, Richard, 170n
prayer, 166, 167
preceptive will, 22n, 44, 109–12,
    167
precepts, 109n
predestination, 86
presentism, 193
presuppositions, 46
Pribham, Karl, 150n

Prime Mover, 29, 32
Pringle-Pattison, Andrew Seth, 37
problem of evil, 68, 105, 123n, 134–41, 209
process theology, 29, 33, 38, 123, 186
procession analogy, 155
prophecy, 67n, 167–70, 199–200
propitiation, 208
providence, 62, 102, 103n, 185

randomness, 28, 93
redemption, 102, 140, 207–8
Reformed theologians, on will of God, 109–10
regeneration, 80
relativity, 150–51
repentance, 79, 166, 196
responsibility, 121
rhetoric, 19–21
Rice, Richard, 21–23, 121
    on divine love, 53–54
    on election, 97–98
    on free will, 129
    on openness, 17
    on prophecy, 199–200
Ritschl, A., 50, 52
Roman Catholic theologians, 108

Saint-Cyran, A., 50
salvation, 74–83, 86, 98–99, 174
Samson, 71
Samuel, 168, 201
sanctification, 82
Sanders, John, 21n, 26, 33, 87, 89–93, 102, 195n, 206
    on election, 99
    on God's causality, 60n
    on logic, 42–44
    on models, 45–46
    and Socinianism, 34–35
    on the will of God, 106, 112–13, 116
Satan, 30, 186
Saul, 168, 201
science, 62

"significant freedom," 23
sin, 67–73, 140, 207
Skinner, B. F., 30
Socinianism, 32–35, 39, 123, 129, 144
Socinus, Fausto, 33
Socinus, Lelio, 33, 35
sola Scriptura, 26n, 27, 124
space, 149
Spinoza, 30, 37n
spiritual understanding, 81
Stoicism, 30, 32, 181
straightforward exegesis, 47–48, 197
Strimple, Robert, 33–34
"strongest desire," 129n
subconscious, 130n
suffering, 84–85, 138–39, 185
Swinburne, Richard, 148

temporal frustration, 155
Tertullian, 27n
Thales, 29
theology of the cross, 19n
Thornwell, James H., 126n, 145
Tillich, Paul, 33
time, 143–59, 176–78
tradition, 34n
traditionalism, 26n
Trinity, 187–88
two ages, 158

union with Christ, 80
universalizing particulars, 89–95, 140n

Van Til, Cornelius, 27
visible church, 97
Vos, Geerhardus, 157
vulnerability, 19

Ware, Bruce A., 11n, 12–13, 46–47, 139, 208
Warfield, B. B., 84, 189
weakness, 185–87
Wells, H. G., 37
Wesley, Charles, 19n
Westminster Confession of Faith, 133–34, 192n

Westminster Shorter Catechism, 172
Whitehead, Alfred North, 38
will, 121
William of Occam, 144
Wilson, Douglas, 195n
wisdom, 29

Wittgenstein, Ludwig, 152n
Wolterstorff, Nicholas, 145–46,
   147, 149, 157–58
Wright, R. K. McGregor, 120

Zeus, 32

John M. Frame (A.B., Princeton University; B.D., Westminster Theological Seminary; A.M. and M.Phil., Yale University) is professor of systematic theology and philosophy at Reformed Theological Seminary, Orlando campus. He previously taught at Westminster Theological Seminary (Philadelphia) and Westminster Theological Seminary in California. He has written widely in the areas of theology, apologetics, ethics, and worship, including *The Doctrine of the Knowledge of God* and *The Doctrine of God* in the Theology of Lordship series, and *Apologetics to the Glory of God* and *Cornelius Van Til: An Analysis of His Thought.*

Pg 74 - 84
Good summary of salvation,
Grace, & Foreknowledge.

See pg 77
Aseity, chosen, Foreknew etc.
word study

Pg 33 Ariminianism,
Socinians.
Open Theist

Pg 29-30 Libertarianism = man does
the world is under control of a
personal creator'
— Things just happen
— God reacts
— God takes risk